TALMUDIC THINKING

TALMUDIC THINKING

Language, Logic, Law

Jacob Neusner

University of South Carolina Press

Copyright © 1992 University of South Carolina

Published in Columbia, South Carolina, by the
University of South Carolina Press

Manufactured in the United States of America

Library of Congress Cataloging-in-Publication Data

Neusner, Jacob, 1932-
    Talmudic thinking : language, logic, law / Jacob Neusner.
        p.   cm.
    Includes bibliographical references and index.
    ISBN 0–87249–825–5 (alk. paper)
    1. Talmud—Criticism, interpretation, etc.   2. Judaism—History—
Talmudic period, 10–425.   I. Title.
BM504.2.N52   1992
296.2'206—dc20   91-48456

For My Friend and Co-worker
Jill Lones

Contents

Preface

This is a book about writing and the social order. I ask how the way in which people express their ideas relates to the society in which (they perceive) they are living. My premise is that the medium of language serves to convey the message: there is a relationship between how I express my ideas and what I wish to say about the world beyond. We hear the drums of war in Haydn's *Mass in Time of War,* and in the shapes of Picasso's *Guernica* I see the nightmare of Spain in those tragic years. Poets capture the cadence of conflict in the rhythm of words as much as in metaphors. So aesthetics, as much as philosophy, conveys a particular kind of message, one not in words but (in the case of writing) in the choice and arrangement of words. The media of language, logic, and law express the message of the Judaic system, or Judaism, which the greatest writing of Judaism, the Talmud of Babylonia, proposes to convey. In dealing with the Talmud of Babylonia or Bavli, I argue specifically that the document's bilingualism, the composite character of its major units of discourse, and the message—never stated in so many words, but always conveyed by indirection—all bear fundamental messages. Here I examine its language, logic of coherence, and law beyond the laws to show how these messages express in a single and simple way, through the subtle but effective medium of aesthetics (broadly construed), the unarticulated message of this richly detailed writing.

In these pages I address the way in which, for the purposes of portraying the entirety of the social order, its culture and its politics alike, people write in signals an account of their modes of thought and how these are to be replicated anytime and anywhere. I deal in detail with evidence of three matters of fundamental character in the writing of a book: language, logic (defined in a limited way), and law (bearing an equally limited definition in these pages). Selection of language in a multilingual culture, choice and arrangement of compositions in composites of discourse (hence, logic), presentation, in diverse contexts, of uniform and paramount propositions (hence, law)—these aspects of writing turn out to form statements of culture. In the case of the Talmud, moreover, the medium of expression not only portrayed but also imparted particular modes of thought—and, as a matter of fact, furthermore dictated the political consequences of thought: practical logic and applied reason, bearing their own sanctions. The success of the Talmud as the instrument for the shaping of Israel's social order derives from the power of its authors to persuade through argument, compel through the shaping of attitudes, the formation of public policy in one way rather than in some other—and to do so for thirteen hundred years past, and God alone knows for how many centuries to come.

The Bavli demands attention because it is the foundation-document of a social order, a piece of writing that was formed by political-intellectual figures, who proposed to say in a single place how they thought Israel, under God's rule through the Torah as they taught it, should form a political entity and a cogent, albeit composite, society. At stake in this study is the demonstration that the way people formulated their thought responded to the manner in which they perceived the social world they proposed to set forth. The issue of general intelligibility therefore pertains to the interplay between writing and the social order.

The intellectual context in which this sustained enterprise of mine on religion and society (here: religious writing and the social order) finds its place is properly identified by a single name, that of Max Weber, who taught us how to ask about the relationship between ideas and the social order. But Weber's address to Judaism yielded nothing; his *Judaism* today can be read only as a chapter in the thought of Weber, in how he brought a good question to the wrong (not merely improperly mastered) evidence. Had Weber had the imagination to grasp the social significance of the Bavli, he would have worked not on the Old Testament, which in no way told him information pertinent to what he wanted to know—why capitalism sprang not from Judaism (or India, China, or Roman Catholic Christianity) but from Protestant Christianity—but on the Bavli.[1]

---

1. At present, Weber scholarship seems to me to have found nothing interesting to say about Weber's *Ancient Judaism*, because scholars on Weber know nothing about the sources and problems of the history of Judaism and work within long-since-discarded categories, indeed with facts that have lost all standing in informed learning.

But I propose to ask what I conceive to be a more compelling question than one about religion and the origins of capitalism, the Marxist agenda having run its course within the house of intellect. For our purpose, the more interesting question that awaits attention concerns the interplay between literature and society. Does writing respond to, even replicate in some way, the social order, and, if it does, what does such writing look like? In these pages I ask how the aesthetic of a document conveys the conception of the social order that the authors of a document meant to represent—and fully intended to realize.

Now to proceed from context to contents: the Talmud of Babylonia recapitulates a religious system. The generative problematic of that writing directs our attention not to the aesthetics of writing, on which I concentrate here, but to the religion of a piece of writing viewed as a document of faith in the formation of a social order. What is at stake in this account of Talmudic thinking, therefore, is the description, analysis, and interpretation of a religious system. My particular method is to ask how a mode of forming thought and formulating discourse—proposition, evidence, argument, held together in an intelligible formation of rhetoric and logic of cogency—recapitulates the document's authors' program for the social order. In this study of Talmudic thinking, I direct attention to only three components of the Bavli's complex intellectual infrastructure. These are: (1) its use of two languages not only to convey information and ideas but also to signal the status and consequence, within the large framework of discourse, of any given statement; (2) its run-on character and why its authorship pursues so meandering a path as it wanders from point to point; and (3) its capacity to say the same thing about many things, and so to impose upon the diversity of the everyday a single and uniform message. I do not merely refer to or describe the writing at hand. I present it in detail and lead the reader within it. My purpose is to show, in detail and on the spot, precisely how a given document conducts discourse in such a way as to make points of consequence far beyond its own documentary limits.

In part 1, "Language," I deal with the fact that the Talmud is in two languages, Hebrew and Aramaic. I show how the use of each language serves to classify the type of discourse that is underway, so that language preference serves a taxonomic purpose—one that, within discourse, is exceedingly important to holding the entire discussion together. In part 2, "The Logic of Coherent Exposition," I address the fact that, whether studied in Hebrew and Aramaic, or read in English, the Talmud rightly strikes readers as meandering and not well focused. It seems to move aimlessly, from point to point, making a diversity of points not required by the initial and governing proposition that generates a sustained discourse. In this part I explain how the Talmud's framers have solved a problem of the limitations of their medium—long columns of undifferentiated words, with no punctuation, no footnotes and the like—by their method of what seems to be incoherent exposition.

In part 3, "The Law behind the Laws," I ask the same question with which I deal in *Judaism as Philosophy*, (Columbia: University of South Carolina Press, 1991), namely, Does the Talmud say different things about everything, or does it say some one thing about everything it treats, and, if so, what is that one thing? I review part of what I said about the Mishnah in *Judaism as Philosophy* and then point out some of the things that I think the Talmud means to say, whatever the subject under discussion.

In this book I translate into results of broad cultural concern some of the findings of recent works of mine, especially of two monographs just now completed, *Language as Taxonomy: The Rules for Using Hebrew and Aramaic in the Babylonian Talmud* (Atlanta: Scholars Press for South Florida Studies in the History of Judaism, 1990) and *The Rules of Composition of the Talmud of Babylonia* (Atlanta: Scholars Press for South Florida Studies in the History of Judaism, 1991). Part 4 of this book further adumbrates analytical studies underway not only in *Rules of Composition* but also in *The Bavli's One Voice: Types and Forms of Analytical Discourse and their Fixed Order of Appearance* (Atlanta: Scholars Press for South Florida Studies in the History of Judaism, 1991).[2]

---

2. Other pertinent monographs of mine are these: *How the Bavli Shaped Rabbinic Discourse* (Atlanta: Scholars Press for South Florida Studies in the History of Judaism, 1991); *The Bavli's Massive Miscellanies: The Problem of Agglutinative Discourse in the Talmud of Babylonia* (Atlanta: Scholars Press for South Florida Studies in the History of Judaism,

Since this is one of the first books I have completed in my new position at the University of South Florida, it is still appropriate that I express my genuine pleasure at the opportunity offered to me here for learning, through both teaching and scholarly inquiry. Ponce de Leon came to these shores seeking youth; I too came to find a kind of healing—not youth, to be sure, for who would trade now for then!—but, unlike him, I have found what I was seeking: renewal. I take pride in my new position and pleasure in my new colleagues and friends. I express thanks to the University of South Florida for generous support for certain research expenses as well. The University's commitment to supporting the research of its teaching faculty sets the standard for the academy in the accomplishment of its single tasks, in two media: re-examination of what we think we know, re-presentation, to the future that is embodied in our students, of what is in our judgment worth knowing:

1992); *Sources and Traditions: Types of Composition in the Talmud of Babylonia* (Atlanta: Scholars Press for South Florida Studies in the History of Judaism, 1992); *The Law behind the Laws: The Bavli's Essential Discourse* (Atlanta: Scholars Press for South Florida Studies in the History of Judaism, 1992); *The Bavli's Primary Discourse: Mishnah Commentary, Its Rhetorical Paradigms and Their Theological Implications in the Talmud of Babylonia Tractate Moed Qatan* (Atlanta: Scholars Press for South Florida Studies in the History of Judaism, 1992); *The Discourse of the Bavli: Language, Literature, and Symbolism: Five Recent Findings* (Atlanta: Scholars Press for South Florida Studies in the History of Judaism, 1991); and *How to Study the Bavli: The Languages, Literatures, and Lessons of the Talmud of Babylonia* (Atlanta: Scholars Press for South Florida Studies in the History of Judaism, 1992). As is clear, I have been working on the pieces of a large puzzle, piece by piece. The present book translates into the issues of general intelligibility what I conceive to be three of the main results.

true and also useful knowledge, learning that addresses issues of consequence.

Since, as every professor knows, by "the University" we mean, and must mean, the people who run the place, I speak of my chairman, dean, provost, and president. They form models of professionalism, and, besides that, are lovely people, whom I admire and appreciate. I have known other chairmen, deans, provosts, and presidents, so through harsh experience have learned to distinguish incompetent from able, destructive from effective, mean-spirited and envious from public-spirited and generous. These are not traits of the profession of academic admiration but gifts of the spirit, so I pay my tribute to my two chairmen at South Florida, William C. Tremmel and James Strange; my dean, Rollin Richmond; my provost, G. G. Meisels; and my president, Francis Borkowski. Still, I do maintain the theory that public education finds the kind of leadership it must have, and private education, in the Ivy League (the only private university system I have ever known, represented by Brown University) also gets what it wants—and deserves.

TALMUDIC THINKING

What Is at Stake, for Understanding Culture and Politics, in Talmudic Thinking?

All religions may be divided into two kinds, those that focus upon immediate experience, and the ones that mediate the everyday through the prism of a long past. Believers in the former expect to, and do, enjoy an immediate encounter with God. Believers in the latter meet God in books as well. What happens in the here and now is shaped by what, to begin with, those books teach them to expect to find. All religions, further, may be divided into two other categories, those that address a select group, identified out of a larger society, and those that set forth an account of the social order that encompasses an entire society. Believers in the former in general attend to the concerns of their group in particular, and issues of consequence in the end derive from a rather private agenda. Believers in the latter treat as critical matters of public policy that concern the ordering of the well-ordered society that their religion proposes to set forth. Within the limitations of literacy, the former kind of religion may or may not meet God in holy books. But the latter type always does, since, as a matter of fact, the representation of the entirety of the social order by its nature will impose the duty of putting everything together and writing everything down in some coherent manner, whether as a law code, a prophecy that in messages from God on political subjects or economic attitudes addresses the here and now, or in some other kind of writing, of general intelligibility, upon the social order.

Every Judaism, past to present, appeals to not only the immediate experience but also to received and authoritative writings that set forth, and make accessible, inherited religious experience as well. Beginning with the Judaism of the Pentateuch composite, some Judaisms, by no means all of them, have moreover formulated their Judaisms in terms of the politics of the social order. These Judaisms set forth their worldview, defined their way of life, and delineated their "Israel," the name, in every Judaism, of the social entity that understands itself by appeal to the worldview and that realizes the way of life, in documents of broad social vision and concern. That is to say, many Judaisms have understood "Israel" to be a political entity, fully empowered; delineated the way of life of their "Israel" as an economic unit, responsible for the proper interchange, within a specified rationality, of scarce resources (however these may have been identified); and portrayed their "Israel" as the embodiment of a philosophical or a theological imperative. Those Judaisms then set forth systems that concerned themselves with the entire order of things: Israel in relationship to all the nations, the castes of Israel in relationship to one another; the proper definition and conduct of the social unit, the household, which also formed the economic unit; the uses of legitimate power, sanctions to preserve order, rewards for sustaining it. These Judaisms in writing therefore put forth prescriptions for the affairs of that "Israel" understood, wherever it was located, as a free-standing political entity—in our language, a nation-society-culture-church.

One of those Judaisms of the latter classification, by far the most important one, the Judaism of the dual Torah, moreover produced a book, the Talmud of Babylonia or Bavli, that was meant to set forth all together and all at once that way of life, worldview, theory of "Israel,"—that account of not only Israel's, but the world's, social order and purpose under God's rule. The Talmud served as the constitution and bylaws of the Israel of whom that Judaism spoke. It portrayed the way of life and it set forth the worldview of that Judaism. As a matter of fact, the Talmud from the time of its closure in approximately A.D. 600, just before the Muslim conquest of the Middle East, North Africa, and much of southern and western Europe, until the nineteenth century, accomplished the goals of its writers. It did define the social order for nearly the whole of its "Israel."

That remarkable record of success—the envy of any writer interested in issues of politics in relationship to culture and religion—finds few counterparts. Among political writings of surpassing theoretical interest, Plato's *Republic*, Aristotle's *Politics*, to name two important documents, influenced many thinkers, but no constitution copied Plato's republic, and no politics responded to

Aristotle's wonderful theory of the whole. Nor did More's *Utopia* provide for anyone a model of how to write up the rules of a state. Among law codes, few single documents—Justinian's is one, Napoleon's another—compete with the Talmud as an enduring and ubiquitously influential statement of the law through the specification of the laws. Since the Talmud set forth not only decisions in right array but also portrayed in intimate exemplary detail the compelling model of correct modes of thought, a further comparison is in order. Among theories of human behavior, properly construed, formulations of ethics and, even more, the modes of thought and analysis by which right decisions are reached, we ask for counterparts but find none. Accounts of right thinking about right action in the formation of public policy and private behavior of the scope and dimensions of the Talmud's account—Plato's dialogues, for instance—do not measure up to the Talmud's in three indicative matters.

First, the Talmud shows how practical reason does its work to make diverse issues and actions conform to a single principle. Second, the Talmud shows how applied logic discerns the regular and the orderly in the confusion and disorder of everyday conflict. Third, the Talmud portrays the right way of thinking about problems that may be worked out in many different analytical modes. Where are we to find massive displays of applied logic and practical reasoning in the analysis of the minutia of the workaday world, showing in the everyday the intimations of regularity, order, compelling purpose, that, all together, point to the governance of a reasonable Creator of an orderly and sensible creation — nature and social order alike? In the Talmud, but not in many other writings.

That fact draws our attention to the importance of writing. The generative question here is this: precisely how do authors who set forth to write a document bearing so grave a responsibility, so lofty an ambition, as the Talmud actually write? If we wonder how practical visionaries, men of learning but also of affairs, propose to say everything in one place in the way in which the authors of the Talmud said everything about the politics of the social order in a single document, here is one of the few occasions for finding an answer. To define the challenge, we should ask for a solution to the following problem: A hundred years after the founding of the American nation, roughly at the turn of the twentieth century, we are asked to take the Constitution of the United States of America and the first ten amendments, *The Federalist* essays, the decisions of the Supreme Court down to *Marbury v. Madison* (the judges' notes as well), the *Congressional Record* of that age, and the *United States Code*; to collect, as well, the corresponding documents of the Presbyterian Church and its synods; to add to the task a respectable selection of the writings of Benjamin Franklin, Washington Irving, Henry David Thoreau, and Ralph Waldo Emerson; and, having mastered the whole, write in a single document everything that we have learned — in such a way as to show future readers how we have reached our conclusions and why these conclusions are compelling and ineluctable.

That formidable task must then begin with a solution to the problem of writing: precisely how do we propose to take over and reshape in discourse that compels assent so varied a legacy? How are we going to give purpose and structure and order to materials that share a common theme—the creation of the United States of America—but little else? This bare-bones account of what I, in their terms and context, conceive the authors of the Bavli to have accomplished defines the problem of this book. The data are technical and detailed. But for the culture and politics of writing, what is at stake is weighty and broadly intelligible.

What makes possible the analysis of the document as a whole is a simple fact. It is that the Talmud in its thirty-seven tractates is entirely uniform, and the stylistic preferences exhibited on any given page characterize every other page of the document. That same fact justifies my insistence that the document's author's or authors' indicative traits of mind, as conveyed in the rules of communication, attest to a vision of a shared realm of discourse, a shared existence, the social order imagined but also portrayed. When people everywhere, whatever the subject or problem, turn out to speak in the same way, and, as we shall see, even to say the same thing about many things, they certainly attract attention to the distinctive traits of expression that they deem correct throughout. What we find on one page we find on every other page, the same rhetoric, the same logic, the same law underlying laws. When, therefore, we examine a single page or a single chapter, we see the entirety of the writing. Given its massive dimensions, then, we are on firm ground in asking about that textual community that has in such a uniform way communicated its message through its method.

When we realize that that community's writing ultimately imposed its method, as much as its message, upon the social world to which its authors proposed to speak, we understand how full and rich is that resource of culture contained within the writing before us. Reaching closure around A.D. 600, the Bavli, with its ongoing discourse of continuous, intimate commentary, magisterial code, and concrete, niggling application through centuries afterward, defined the world order of Judaism. From the end of late antiquity at the rise of Islam to nearly the present day, that one writing defined Judaism. The intellectual foundations of social action, the beliefs and values of culture, the national consensus that defined ways of forming family and conducting everyday life, the ethos and ethics of the diverse people of Israel, wherever they lived, responded to—and aimed to realize in concrete ways—the religious system set forth in that vast document. If, therefore, we wish to understand the relationship between the ideas people hold and the world they make for themselves, we find in that Talmud an example rich in promise.

For writing, as people now appreciate, not only sets forth messages through the statement of propositions. Writing also bears signification through how things are said, indeed, perhaps in a more effective and profound way than through what is said. If, therefore, we wish to move from writing to the world that that writing is meant to adumbrate, formulate, portray, and even—in word and sound, then in deed and fact—realize, we will do well to pay close attention to a document that made the world its authors intended to make. Moreover, that world came to realization within the intellectual life of the very readers whom the authors proposed to influence and shape. Few documents in the entire history of the West—the Bible created by Christianity is one, the writings of Aristotle another—have so informed and shaped society in the way in which, within the community of Israel, the Jewish people, the Bavli did. So in the study of the relationship of ideas and society, writing and the message communicated and realized through writing, this document bears special interest.

This is why the manner of writing may instruct us on matters of general intelligibility and public consequence. And when we deal with a document that itself is intended as a plan for the conduct of life of an entire society, and which in time was realized, we understand that what are at stake are considerable concerns of culture. So while we pay close attention to some rather arcane and technical problems in a remote and unfamiliar piece of writing, in these pages we see how modes of thought themselves convey—and effect—social, indeed even public policy. Language, the logical representation of coherent thought, the representation of one important thing through many unimportant ones— these traits of a literary culture instruct us on the formation of the social order of the foundation-document that exhibits them. Through them the textual community frames the social order.

We deal in particular with a document remarkable for its power to define the social order of an entire people, living under diverse rules of politics, culture, economy, and society. Wherever Jews lived from the seventh century to nearly our own time, they found in the Talmud of Babylonia the rules that would govern their social order. What makes the modes of thought of the Talmud important, therefore, is that, through thinking in this way, rather than in some other, people formulated a public policy in the grandest dimensions of their shared lives. What makes those modes of thought accessible is the uniformity of discourse characteristic of the Talmud of Babylonia or Bavli. That uniform discourse produces the recurrence of a few fixed forms and formulas. The rather monotonous, even tedious character of the writing at hand attests to its authorship's adherence to a few rules that prove determinative beginning to end. The document exhibits remarkable integrity; the limits of the document clearly are delineated, and when other documents are introduced in evidence, they too are marked in the manner in which, in this period and within the technical limitations operative then, people were able to cite or place in quotations or footnotes materials borrowed from other sources. This is a writing that does not (merely) allude or hint at something found somewhere else; it articulately cites, it explicitly quotes. Within the limits of the Bavli, the document defines its own infrastructure in both rhetoric and logic. And, as we see, beyond the limits of the writing, the world beyond responded, thinking in one way, and so ordering the affairs of families and communities in the way in which they did, rather than in some order.

Take for example the bilingual character of the writing and the fixed rule that dictates to an author which language serves for what purpose. What do we learn about a document addressed to the formation of society, in which two languages are utilized, each for a particular type of discourse? The question is relevant, because in the Talmud of Babylonia what is said in Hebrew is represented as authoritative and formulates a normative thought or rule. What is said in Aramaic is analytical and commonly signals an argument and formulates a process of inquiry and criticism. This is how language serves a taxonomic purpose. Hebrew is the language of the result; Aramaic, of the way by which the result is achieved. Hebrew is the formulation of the decision; Aramaic, of the work of deliberation. Each language serves to classify what is said in that language, and we always know where we stand, in a given process of thought and the exposition of thought, by reference to the language used at that particular place in the sustained discourse to which we are witness. That fixed rule, utilizing language for the purpose of classifying what is said in that language, characterizes only one document in the canon of Judaism, and that is the Talmud.[1] All other canonical documents are

---

1. I refer of course to the Talmud of Babylonia. I have not analyzed the Talmud of the Land of Israel in the same way. The comparison of

monolingual, ordinarily in Hebrew, so that, where Aramaic occurs, it is generally a brief allusion to something deemed external to what the author wishes to say in his own behalf, for example, a citation of everyday speech, invariably assumed to be in Aramaic.[2]

When we know the rules of composition of thought, the issues that would arise in response to any topic that would be treated, the analytical questions that would be addressed without regard to subject matter, the premises of all inquiry—the fixed outlines of all intellect—we know how thought was framed, formulated, and conveyed. And when we understand the rules of composition defined in this way, we also can move from detail to main point, holding together within a single descriptive framework the myriad of details that served the Bavli's authors and framers in making the few fundamental points that they wished to make. These I call rules of composition, meaning the forming of large-scale composites. These cover not only correct usage of language, the grammar of (socially, contextually) proper and educated expression, but also something of more profound weight. I refer to the rules that dictate the conven-

---

the two Talmuds can take place only when the Bavli has been fully characterized. My preliminary reading of matters is in *Judaism: The Classical Statement: The Evidence of the Bavli* (Chicago: University of Chicago Press, 1986).

2. Obviously, within the canon of the Judaism of the dual Torah, some of the translations of the Hebrew Scriptures into Aramaic, or Targumim, are canonical; others are not. The standing of other Aramaic writings, such as Sefer Harazim or Megillat Taanit, remains to be worked out.

tions of thought by defining the accepted conventions of expression. "The limits of my language are the limits of my world" in this context means that how I express myself properly tells me what I may properly think about. In a writing of an analytical character, rules of composition dictate the repertoire of appropriate questions, indicating what issues demand sustained attention and (implicitly) which ones may be ignored.

These rules of composition in the Talmud of Babylonia, a remarkably uniform and conceptually simple writing, were few, readily learned, and easily discerned. One who knows the rules of expression—and anyone who has studied a sufficient volume of the document knows the rules implicitly, even though he or she may not grasp every detail of their application to an articulated case—always is able to define the analytical context, define an appropriate solution to a properly framed problem, answer a question to the point, and grasp both the point and what is at stake in the question. Rules of composition therefore were not merely formal rules of correct arrangement of various classifications of words (e.g., nouns, verbs); they encompassed more than correct usage of language in such a way that how things were said would be socially acceptable and intellectually comprehensible. Rules of composition always involved recurrent forms, but—and this must be fully appreciated—while formal and routine, they were never mere formalities, and they were never to be distinguished from the substance of things.

For the rules of composition in the Bavli governed not only how a writer (or formulator of a thought for oral transmission) would make his statement, but also what he would say. Rules of composition place limitations upon thought for the purpose of communication within a given society, for the medium ubiquitously dictates the message in any determinate context, and the document before us, deriving as it did from a textual community of a clearly defined and limited order, set forth its messages not only through what was said about some specific subject, but through how anything might be said about any subject that came under consideration. Anyone who has studied a large sample of the Talmud of Babylonia will readily list a variety of fixed syntactic forms, on the one side, and a substantial catalog of examples of how a great many subjects are formulated within that limited variety of syntactic forms, on the other.

What I shall show in these pages, therefore, is a very simple fact about a document that, in the aggregate, has been crafted in an entirely accessible way. When we understand the rules of composition that govern which language to use for what purpose and how to form connections between one thing and something else in a composition that in all its complexity bears a message—we take a long step toward the explanation of the social order that the document's heirs constructed on the foundation of a writing that is written in one way rather than in some other—a way the rules of which we can delineate and explain. While subject to much obfuscation, in fact the Talmud of Babylonia is an accessible document, because its authors followed rules which we can discern and employ in our reading of this writing. While the writing sometimes appears run-on, with a subject shifting and then changing again, when we understand why that is so, the document appears entirely cogent. Further, while the topical program of the writing covers a long list of subjects, we shall see that a few points are made over and over again, without regard to the subject under discussion. We gain access to Talmudic thinking, therefore, when we examine the method of the writers, not only their message. And when we do, that method turns out to impart cogency to the writing as a whole—with profound consequences for our reading of the document as a statement of the social order of Judaism.

Part One

Language

Chapter 1

Language as Taxonomy: The Intratextuality of the Talmud

> In rabbinic Judaism the writing and discourse of scripture had to be inherently separable from, and could be neither merged nor confused with, the commentary upon them. . . . The rabbinic tendency to identify antecedent materials is not limited to scripture . . . the adjectives "allusive" and "intertextual" are analytically useless for a critical description of rabbinic hermeneutics . . . rabbinic literature displays its sources.
>
> William Scott Green[1]

The Bavli is written in two languages, Hebrew and Aramaic. Where Hebrew is used, it is ordinarily for the purpose of setting forth facts deriving from authoritative writings, on the one side, or authoritative figures, on the other. Where Aramaic is used, it is ordinarily for the purpose of analyzing facts, though it may serve also to set forth cases that invariably are subordinated to the analytical task. The simple fact that in the pages of the Bavli the same figures "speak" in both Hebrew and Aramaic proves that at stake is not merely "how peo-

---

1. See his "Writing with Scripture: The Rabbinic Uses of the Hebrew Bible," in Jacob Neusner with William Scott Green, *Writing with Scripture: The Authority and Uses of the Hebrew Bible in the Torah of Formative Judaism* (Minneapolis: Fortress Press, 1989), 17.

ple said things,"let alone *ipissima verba*; if the master Yohanan in the Land of Israel or the masters Samuel and Rab in Babylonia are sometimes represented as speaking in Hebrew and other times in Aramaic, the function served by using the two languages, respectively, must form the point of inquiry into how and why these languages are used where and when they make their appearance. The choice of language clearly conveys part of the message the authorship means to set forth, signaling to the reader precisely what is happening at any given point. Along these same lines, a story, told in Aramaic, yields a formulation of a general rule or conclusion, presented in (Middle) Hebrew. The upshot is that the language in which a statement is made classifies that statement, telling me precisely its status and function in a larger composite discourse—hence, language as taxonomy.

It follows that in the Talmud of Babylonia the choice of language therefore carried a particular message, one of classification. A reader or listener who read or heard Aramaic immediately knew what kind of discourse was underway, and when Hebrew was used, the reader or listener forthwith understood the status and purpose of the discourse, which was then subject to representation.[2]

---

2. The distinction between written and oral prose is a valid one, but it forms no part of the argument of this book. It is clear that a great many things were memorized within the process of formulating and transmitting the Bavli; it is equally clear that, at a given point, things were written down. I am not sure where or why what was formulated orally was written down. My impression is that the document was written down very early in the process of its composition, and that people who formulated composites drew upon

The selection of one language over another gave the signal that sayings, and, more to the point, whole paragraphs and even long and sustained passages, in one language were to be classified in one way, and sayings or entire compositions in another, in a different way. And that taxonomic function served by the choice of language bore no relationship to the circumstances of time, place, and personality, let alone the original words that were said; the same named speakers are given statements in two languages, depending on the purpose served by a given statement within the unfolding of discourse.

What is at stake in these facts? Finding a parallel for guidance proves difficult, for a political foundation-document of society in two or more languages, both accorded equal honor but each serving its own purpose, is not easy to locate. One analogy would be the composition of the United States Constitution in English, the *United States Code* in Latin; but that hardly serves, since, as we shall see, the power of Aramaic in the Talmud takes effect in the *how* of thought, not the *what* of what is said. A further analogy, the use of Latin for law and judgment, and a vernacular for chitchat, obviously does not serve, for, as we shall see, that language of conversation and argument, Aramaic, serves side by side, within the same paragraph, with the official language, Mishnaic-Hebrew, and,

---

materials that came to them through the memories of official memorizers. But that problem of the literary history of the Bavli is not under study in these pages.

more tellingly, the same people who speak in Aramaic also say things in Hebrew. In a profound sense the two languages work together to make a single statement, which is coherent at every point, so the analogy of the use of Latin for one document, the vernacular for an intertwined one, will not serve very well. The Bavli, then, requires inspection on its own terms and in acute detail, there being no obvious analogy to its distinctive bilingualism. And anyone interested in modes of thought conveyed through the utilization of language in any event will want to see at all the fine points precisely what this set of writers have done with the instrument of bilingualism to make their single and utterly unitary statement.

Bilingualism communicated with great effect in the Bavli. A principal trait of the Bavli (and of the entirety of the canon that reaches its conclusion in the Bavli) is stress on the distinction between that authoritative document and prior, also authoritative documents. The authorship of any document in the canon of the Judaism of the dual Torah invariably insisted on identifying its authorities. These were authorships addicted to footnotes, meticulous about differentiating their statements from those of their predecessors (and masters). What signal did they give by setting off their own statements from those made by others, in their own time and also in times past?[3] By engaging in the

---

3. Since the paramount trait of the Bavli is its propensity to cite its sources, e.g., "as it is said" or " . . . written" for Scripture, and "as

task of interpreting and reshaping in their own
names what they had inherited from the authoritative past,[4] those same authorships established
themselves as authoritative—themselves as wor-
thy of participating in an ongoing exchange and
interchange, even with Sinai. The importance of
citing the past derived from the purpose of
attribution and explicit citation—a purpose to be
achieved only through highlighting the act of citation or quotation. It was to deal with what was

---

has been taught on Tannaite authority" for authoritative statements
of the Mishnah, Tosefta, or figures bearing the standing of those
writings, I am unable to understand some scholars' characterization of the rabbinic writers as having produced what is called "intertextual" writing. My impression is that my colleagues who
portray Midrash or Talmud writings as intertextual have made their
commitment to the hermeneutic of intertextuality and brought that
mode of reading to the document at hand, intending to find in it an
ancient, distinctively Jewish (not merely Judaic) precedent for their
acutely modern way of reading writing. Their portrayal of matters
certainly does not derive from a deep and careful, meticulous and
detailed reading of the entirety of the literature, such as I have produced in the monographic corpus the results of which in part are
set forth here.

4. The precise assignment of most of what is said to named authorities, with close attention to the sources of those authorities in prior
masters, attests once again to the opposite of an intertextualist
mode of forming and setting forth writing. Indeed, while I can explain, within my intratextualist representation of the writing, precisely what is at stake in the careful identification of the names of
speakers, I wonder how, within the intertextualist position, people
can make any sense at all of delineating this one's words from that
one's! It is not a problem that seems to have impressed the intertextualist readers of the rabbinic canon, even though the constant
attribution of statements must impress any reader of the Bavli as
one of its indicative traits, and one that demands explanation. Perhaps in the end intertextualism will lose out because of the data it
does not explain, even more than because of its utter misrepresen-
tation of the facts of the writing it claims to interpret.

cited, to impose upon the citation an acutely contemporary significance and meaning. This intervention—not just paraphrase and pious rewording, but the explicit setting forth of its own opinion upon an issue within the framework of the received text—laid claim in behalf of the current generation to join the conversation begun at Sinai. In the intratextuality of the Bavli we deal with a way in which an authority joined in the work of formulating and transmitting the Torah not only in writing, but also in memory, orally.

By constantly referring to earlier writings deemed revealed by God to Moses at Sinai, beginning with Scripture, the authorship of the Bavli therefore identified the reason people should conform to its teachings. They constantly proposed to demonstrate that opinions on issues which they identified and formulated in their own language and wording conformed to principles set forth in the written Torah at Sinai. But authority was not vested in Sinai alone. By consistently assigning to the names of near-at-hand authorities statements made in the context of the analysis of received truths, as much as by preserving the articulated distinction between those earlier, revealed writings and the writing at hand, those same authorities identified their own part in the long-term process. They long ago said that . . . , and, in conformity with revealed truth, we, here and now, for our part, in our words, in our language, in our formulation, say this. . . .

Thus, by the articulated differentiation between what they now said and what Scripture had said, they established not the discontinuity but the continuity between their writing and the earlier ones. They showed that they were not merely epigones but participants: "we can back up what we say in prior, revealed writings, but, for our part, we too have a say." It is by that subtle but critical message—authoritative by appeal to received revelation, authoritative by participation in a process of revelation, but also authoritative on one's own part—that the document accounted for the continuity of the civilization that it proposed to compose. Authority came down from the past, but authority also was exercised by the living generation, not only in relationship to the past but on its own, in continuity with the past. And, as we shall see, the part in Aramaic, that is, the acutely contemporary statement, formed the analytical continuum, sorting out and sifting the received aphoristic formulations in Hebrew. So far as sharp logic served to select sense out of received truth, it was the statement of the Aramaic voice—our voice, the authors' voice.

The right to speak forms a powerful claim of authority: to speak in one's own name, not only to cite or quote or allude to what has been said in the past. Critical, analytical thinking validates that claim and confers that right. Factual truth then comes in Hebrew; the applied logic and practical reason that select from truth what is relevant and useful to a particular case come to expression in Aramaic. We may say that, in general, those negotiators of culture who dispose of the past do so either by indirection or explicitly; the former refer, reso-

nate, negotiate, and accommodate. The latter cite
but also say what they think, as well. The relationship of the former to the received literature, in literary terms, is to be characterized as intertextual;
the relationship of the latter, as intratextual. The
former alludes to, the latter quotes. The former im-
plies, producing inferences; the latter states, drawing conclusions. The former speaks by indirection
and in a subtle way; the latter delivers the message
of citation articulately, always with the quotation
marks supplied by "as it is said," or "as it is written," reenforced by "Rabbi X says Rabbi Y says,"
or "Rabbi X says, and some say, Rabbi Y says."

As between the intertextual and the intratextual
relationships to the received and authoritative documents of the past, the authorship of the Bavli
stood in an entirely intratextual relationship with
the Scriptures or written Torah, the Mishnah, and
the other, prior compilations classified in due
course as the oral Torah. This statement of auton-
omy and this relationship of intratextuality reached
expression not only in what people said but also in
how they said it—down to the selection of the language used for their own ideas: Scripture was in
what we generally call biblical Hebrew; the Mishnah and the rest of the corpus assigned to authorities of the Mishnah, in Mishnaic or Middle
Hebrew. And, as a natural next step beyond the
linguistic differentiation present at the very foundations, the Bavli utilized language difference to
signal other fundamental difference as well. Moving from verses of Scripture, in biblical Hebrew, to
statements of Mishnah authorities, in Mishnaic

Hebrew, the authorship of the Bavli turned to Aramaic as the language that signified their commanding presence within the total statement they set forth. And that language established a paramount, dominant, and remarkable presence indeed: the voice of the document, their voice.

True enough, language alone did not bear the entire burden of differentiation, as Green has stressed; they nearly always made it clear that, when a verse of Scripture was at hand, it would be carefully differentiated from what they themselves had to say. They not only alluded to Scripture here and there; when Scripture played a critical role in discourse, it was explicitly cited, by routinely and ubiquitously using such language as "as it is said," or "as it is written." In those nearly universal signals the authorities of the Talmud of Babylonia separated their statements from those of Scripture. But, further, by their choice of the very language in which they would express what they wished to say on their own account, they differentiated themselves from their antecedents. When it came to citations from prior, non-scriptual authorities, they used one formation of the Hebrew language, specifically, Middle, or Mishnaic, Hebrew; when it came to the conduct of their own analytical process, they used one formation of the Aramaic language, Eastern or Talmudic Aramaic. They never alluded to authoritative facts, but always cited them in so many words; but the indication of citation—in a writing in which the modern sigla of quotation marks and footnotes were simply unavailable—came to expression in the choice of language. Green's rejection of "allusive" and "intertextual" as adjectives for the characterization of rabbinic hermeneutics is further validated by the fact that the Talmud of Babylonia not only was not intertextual, but was, as we shall see, uniformly and wholly intratextual.

The infrastructure of the Bavli, its entire repertoire of editorial conventions and sigla, are in Aramaic. When a saying is assigned to a named authority, the saying may be in Hebrew or in Aramaic, and the same named authority may be given sayings in both languages—even within the same sentence. But the editorial and conceptual infrastructure of the document comes to expression only in Aramaic, and when no name is attached to a statement, that statement is always in Aramaic, unless it forms part of a larger, autonomous Hebrew composition cited by, or parachuted down into, "the Talmud." Rightly have the Talmudic masters in the Yeshiva world hypostatized the Talmud in such language as, "the Gemara says . . . ," because the Talmud speaks in a single voice, forms a unitary discourse, beginning, middle, and end, and constitutes one wholly coherent and cogent document, everywhere asking questions drawn from a single determinate and limited repertoire of intellectual initiatives—and always framing those questions, pursuing those inquiries, in Aramaic.

And yet, as everybody knows, the Talmud also is full of Hebrew. So we must ask where and why framers of this writing utilize the Hebrew language, and when we may expect to find that they speak—

rather, "the Talmud speaks"—in Aramaic. Specifically, what signal is given, what purpose is served by the bi-or multilingualism of the Talmud? What do we know without further ado, when we are given a composition or a component of a composition in Hebrew, and what is the implicit meaning of making a statement in Aramaic? The answer is that the choice of language signals a taxonomic meaning, so that language serves as a medium for the classification of discourse, hence, the title of this chapter, Language as Taxonomy. In a writing that utilizes two languages,[5] the choice of one over the other conformed to rules of communication and marked what was said as one type of statement rather than another. If we know which language is used, we also know where we stand in the expression of thought, and the very language in which a statement is made therefore forms

---

5. Really, four: biblical and Middle or Mishnaic Hebrew, Eastern Aramaic in the Talmud of Babylonia, Palestinian Aramaic in the Talmud of the Land of Israel. But in these pages I am interested only in gross taxonomic traits, hence merely the undifferentiated reference to "Hebrew" and "Aramaic." In point of fact, the preservation of citations of the Hebrew Scriptures in biblical Hebrew, rather than their translation into Aramaic, and the formulation of a given part of the document in Eastern rather than Palestinian Aramaic, such as was used in the Talmud of the Land of Israel, also represent important decisions on the part of writers. But my interest here is limited to the gross taxonomic function served by the principal language groups, rather than their subdivisions as well. A study of the relationship between the Talmud of the Land of Israel and the Talmud of Babylonia, particularly of how the latter reworks what it receives from the former, will pay attention to the two kinds of Aramaic that were available to our writers. That is not my problem here.

part of the method of thought and even the message of discourse of the document.

While Hebrew and Aramaic served a single piece of writing, that does not mean that the authorship addressed two different audiences. To the contrary, authors of compositions, framers of composites, and, it surely was assumed, those who would hear or read the document later on, all took for granted knowledge of both languages. That is proved by the simple fact that what is in Hebrew is not then paraphrased in Aramaic, or vice versa; so the authors took for granted that everybody understood everything. Moreover, the linguistic differences were not merely matters of word choice, e.g., a Hebrew phrase or technical term introduced into an Aramaic sentence, or a Hebrew sentence of a legal, formulary character parachuted down into an Aramaic paragraph, though both phenomena prove common. Rather, one type of discussion, serving one purpose, would appear in Aramaic, and another, quite different type of statement, serving (in this context) a quite different purpose, would appear in Hebrew. The pattern is consistent throughout, which allows us, by simple observation and induction, to conclude that quite simple rules instructed the writer of a composition for the Talmud of Babylonia which language to use for a given purpose.

To make matters concrete, I give two brief samples of how a single passage conforms to the simple rules I have described. The first shows us how the bilingualism of the document sorts matters out for us, so that we always know where we stand;

the second gives us the same masters speaking in two languages, each for its own purpose. The Mishnah paragraph is given in boldface type, Aramaic in italics, Hebrew in regular type. The first case is the simplest. The point of the composition, toward which the author is aiming, is in Aramaic. The sustaining voice—asking, answering, probing—speaks in Aramaic. The facts under discussion are in Hebrew; these facts are identified as to source (e.g., Mishnah, Tosefta, Scripture), being set off, as Green insists, from the document's authors' utilization of them; our authors do not allude to a shared corpus of facts or truths, though they obviously take for granted the omnipresence of such a corpus; they explicitly and articulately cite items out of that corpus, and, as we shall now see, when they shift language, it serves the purpose of quotation marks or footnotes (media for signification not available to the authors who either formulated and transmitted their composition or composite orally, or who wrote things down, or who found some intermediary medium for the fixed preservation of their thought, and the distinctions make no difference so far as the taxonomic power of language is concerned). The first example and the simplest derives from Bavli Bekhorot dealing with Mishnah Bekhorot 4:1–2:[6]

---

6. All translations are my own. My mode of presentation of the original sources should be explained. Readers unfamiliar with the Bavli will readily perceive that each sustained discourse in what follows here begins with a passage of the Mishnah, which I give entirely in boldface type, followed by a sequence of composite discussions of sentences of the Mishnah paragraph at hand. Passages of the To-

IV.1 A. **[If] a blemish appeared in it during its first year, it is permitted to keep it for the whole twelve months. [If a blemish appeared in it] after its first year, it is permitted to keep it only for thirty days:**

B. *The question was raised: What is the sense of this passage?* When it says, **[If] a blemish appeared in it during its first year, it is permitted to keep it for the whole twelve months,** *does it mean,* and an additional thirty days as well? Or perhaps the sense is, **[If] a blemish appeared in it during its first year, it is permitted to keep it for the whole twelve months**—*but no longer, and* **[If a blemish appeared in it] after its first year, it is permitted to keep it only for thirty days?**

---

sefta, a large complement to the Mishnah made of up materials represented as deriving from the same authorities for whom the Mishnah speaks, are given in boldface type as well. The Talmud proper then follows the Mishnah, made up of distinct parts. These long discussions, between one Mishnah paragraph and the next, are broken up by my reference system (there is no other detailed reference system for any document of the entire canon of Judaism in the formative age into units bearing a Roman numeral, signifying a sentence of the paragraph cited for discussion; units bearing an Arabic numeral, identifying a complete proposition, beginning, middle, and end; and units bearing a letter, identifying the smallest whole units of thought. These would correspond, in academic writing, to a chapter, a subdivision of a chapter, and a paragraph or very long sentence. Verses of Scripture are set off in quotation marks and identified as to their source. Readers therefore can readily identify the sources that are utilized and the words that are contributed by the Talmud's own authorship. As mentioned above, they can further see at a glance what is in Hebrew, given in regular type, and what is in Aramaic, given in italics. This is how my system of referring to and representing in various typefaces the sources and languages of the document works.

C. *Come and take note, for it has been taught on Tannaite authority:*

D. **At this time [after the destruction of the Temple] a firstling, so long as it is not fit to show to a sage [that is, before there is a blemish on it, to be shown to the sage for a decision on whether it is transient or permanent], may be kept two or three years. Once it is fit to be shown to a sage, if a blemish appeared on it during the first year, he may keep it the entire twelve months. If it was after its first year, he is not allowed to keep it even a single day, even a single hour, but on grounds of restoring what is lost to the owner, rabbis have said that he is permitted to keep the animal for thirty days [T. Bekh. 3:2A–C].**

E. *And still the question is to be raised: does this mean,* thirty days after the first year, *or does it mean* thirty days before its first year is over?

F. *Come and take note:* if a blemish appeared on the beast on the fifteenth day within its first year, we complete it for fifteen days after its first year.

G. *That proves the matter.*

H. *It further supports the position of R. Eleazar, for* R. Eleazar has said, "They assign to the animal thirty days from the moment at which the blemish appeared on the beast."

I. *There are those who say,* said R. Eleazar,"How do we know in the case of a firstling that if a blemish appeared in its first year, we assign to it thirty days after its year? 'You shall eat it before the Lord your God year by year' (Dt. 15:20) [but not in the year in which its blemish has appeared]. Now what is the span of days that is reckoned as a year? You have to say it is thirty days."

J. *An objection was raised:* if a blemish appeared on the beast on the fifteenth day within its first year, we complete it for fifteen days after its first year. *That indicates, then, that we complete the thirty days, but we do not give it thirty full days after the first year, and that would appear to refute the position of R. Eleazar!*

K. *It does indeed refute his position.*

In this example, the way in which the rule I have defined does its work is blatant and, at this stage, merely formal. Where a received document is cited—here, the Mishnah—it is in Hebrew. The language of citation is in Aramaic, so A, B, C, D alternate within that fixed, formal rule. A poor framing of the rule that is implicit then is that we quote in Hebrew, but talk in Aramaic.

But of course recourse to such formalities hardly supplies the key. For the question is asked properly only when we inquire, What guidance do we gain—automatically and implicitly—when we find words framed in Aramaic, and what does the use of Hebrew tell us? The answer cannot concern only the pedantry involved in knowing what comes from where. Who (other than a scholar) would care? The document as a whole is a sustained labor of applied reason and practical logic; it makes important points not only discretely but through the formation of the whole. Its authorship over and over again pursues a single intellectual program, which means that, at every detail, the intellectuals who produced this remarkable document wished to make the same point(s), just as their predecessors did in dealing with the myriad details treated in the Mishnah.[7]

In point of fact, the composition means to pursue a problem, which is formulated at B. And the operative language used in the formulation of the problem is Aramaic, pure and simple. We note at E that fixed formulas in Hebrew are preserved, but Hebrew is not the language of the sentence, any more than, in an American legal brief, the occurrence of a phrase or sentence in Latin signals that the author is writing in Latin; these are conventions of rhetoric or technical terms, nothing more. The continuity and coherence derive from what is said in Aramaic, and that is the case throughout. What we are given in Hebrew then are the facts, the received and established data. When Aramaic appears, it is the voice of the framer of the passage. Since, as a matter of fact, that voice is monotonous and ubiquitous, we realize that it is "the Talmud" that speaks Aramaic, or, in less mythic language, Aramaic is the language of the Talmud, and the use of Hebrew serves a purpose dictated by the document and bears significance within the norms of

---

7. See my *The Philosophical Mishnah*, vols. 1-4 (Atlanta: Scholars Press for Brown Judaic Studies, 1989) and *Judaism as Philosophy: The Method and Message of the Mishnah*. (Columbia: University of South Carolina Press, 1991).

thought that the framers of the document have defined.

In what follows, the same authorities speak in both Hebrew and Aramaic. What they say in Hebrew is a simple law, a fact and a given. What they say in Aramaic is the reason behind the fact, the secondary considerations at play. This fact proves to be decisive evidence that the language choice in no way relates to preferences of individuals but serves a different — taxonomic — I maintain, purpose.

5:4C–G

C. **Any blemishes which are likely to happen at the hands of man —**

D. **Israelite-cast shepherds are believed [to testify that the blemishes came about unintentionally].**

E. **But priestly-cast shepherds are not believed.**

I.1 A. [In reference to the rule, **Israelite-cast shepherds are believed [to testify that the blemishes came about unintentionally]. But priestly-cast shepherds are not believed]**, R. Yohanan and R. Eleazer —

B. One said, **"Israelite-cast shepherds** in the household of priestly-caste shepherds *are* **believed [to testify that the blemishes came about unintentionally].** *We do not take account of the possibility that their testimony is on account of their living.* **But priestly-cast shepherds** in the household of Israelite-caste householders **are not believed.** *The shepherd might say, 'Since I* *work for him, he will not pass me by and give it to someone else.' And the same applies to a priest employed by another priest, for we take account of the possibility of their favoring one another. And Rabban Simeon b. Gamaliel comes to say,* **'He [a priest] is believed concerning another's [firstling] but is not believed concerning his own.'** *And R. Meir comes along to say,* **'He who is suspect in a given matter neither judges nor bears witness in that matter.' "**

C. The other said, "**Shepherds** for Israelites, who are themselves priests **[35B] are believed [to testify that the blemishes came about unintentionally].** *The shepherd will say, 'My employee will not bypass a priest who is a disciple of rabbis to give the firstling to me.'* **But priestly-cast sheep**—meaning, animals belonging to priests, and even if the shepherds are Israelites, **are not believed.** *We take account of the possibility that they may give testimony under the influence of the need to make a living. And all the more so is this the rule when a shepherd of the priestly caste is working for an employer of the priestly caste, for we take account of the possibility of their favoring one another as well as of the possibility that they are concerned about making a living. And Rabban Simeon b. Gamaliel comes to say,* **'He [a priest] is believed concerning another's [firstling] but is not believed concerning his own.'** *And R. Meir comes along to say,* **'He who is suspect in a given matter neither judges nor bears witness in that matter.' "**

Of special interest is the shift from Hebrew to Aramaic at I.1B, C, the rule being in Hebrew, the exposition of the reasoning behind it, in Aramaic. What is important here is the clear evidence that the author knows precisely which language to use for what type of statement, even when the same authority says the whole thing. That proves beyond a doubt that what is in play is not the consideration of who says what and when—e.g., earlier figures talk in Hebrew because they speak Hebrew; later ones, Aramaic. When the same figure speaks both languages, at issue must be something other than historical (or biographical) considerations.

Well, then, perhaps using Hebrew in citations of Scripture or the Mishnah or related materials is simply a medium for preserving what is cited in the original, not part of the system of signals that the authors at hand utilized for the purpose of communicating with their readers. The fact is that Hebrew is used, the very same Hebrew of the Mishnah, when a statement is made which is not Mishnaic or derived from an associated source or authority. A master generally assumed to have lived in the fifth or sixth century will instruct the Tannaite memorizer of his household or school or court to state matters in one way rather than in some other. His instructions always will be presented in Hebrew: say *this* not *that*, and both *this* and *that* are in Hebrew. The use of Hebrew therefore forms part of the conventional substrate of the document, conveying a claim and a meaning, and what it signals is not merely "quoting from the original source," though that is, as a matter of fact, part of the message of facticity, the classification of a statement as a datum, that the use of Hebrew is meant to convey.

What about Aramaic? That too signals not where or when a saying was formulated but the classification of the saying. Where we find Aramaic, the language of sustained discourse, of continuity, cogency, and coherence, it will commonly tell us, through the very choice of language that: (1) a passage formulates an analytical or critical problem and is engaged in solving it; and (2) a passage is particular and episodic—commonly, case reports about things decided in courts of the time of the document are set forth in Aramaic and stories about things authorities have done will be told in Aramaic; these invariably are asked to exemplify a point beyond themselves.

These two purposes for which Aramaic is used on the surface do not entirely cohere. The first is abstract, the second, concrete; the first pursues a problem of theory and calls upon evidence in the service of the sustained process of applied reason and practical logic, while the second signals the presence of thought which is singular and concrete. So if we find a passage in Aramaic, we may stand in two quite unrelated points in the unfolding representation of thought. But, in fact, the second way in which Aramaic may be used invariably finds its place within the framework of a discussion formulated as a sustained process of critical analysis, so the choice of Aramaic for what is episodic turns out not surprising, when we realize that the episode is presented specifically so as to be trans-

formed from an anecdote into a medium of demonstration and proof. The case forms part of an
argument; evidence flows into argument; and all
argument then is in the same language, the Aramaic that forms the language of the document
when the framers of the document speak for themselves and within the process of their own
thought. When they shift to Hebrew, it will signal
either the upshot of analysis, or mutatis mutandis,
the precipitating occasion for analysis.

What takes center stage is not so much what it is
that the (Aramaic) speaker wishes to say but how
the Aramaic speaker chooses to set forth his message: the types of discourse, the forms that repeatedly serve to formulate and signal those types of
discourse, and the order in which those types (and
forms) of discourse make their appearance. When
we can say what is the message of the (linguistic)
medium that communicates with us here, then we
can control for the particularizations of that ubiquitous, infrastructural message. In part three of this
book I shall point to some answers to the question,
what message does the method set forth? But what
about the backward perspective? What I have
shown here for the Bavli is that, as between the
classifications of literary criticism, intertextuality
and intratextuality, the Bavli is to be described as
intratextualist.[8] The reason is that its author or au-

---

8. The term *intertextualism* bears a variety of definitions, but in general
   has been used when literary critics and other scholars of aesthetics
   wished to claim that a writer conceived of work "not as a creation

thors carefully delineate their own document from other documents upon which they draw. What they wish to say is in one language, their other, different (prior, authoritative) sources, in Hebrew.

So the voice of the Bavli, or the Talmud, is the Aramaic voice of applied reason and practical logic—applied to, practiced upon, the Hebrew-language writings (or statements orally formulated and orally transmitted) of the Mishnah and comparable sources. Accordingly, the Bavli forms the pivot. Its authorship's choices present the one solid fact in relationship to which everything else then takes a position relative to that fact. The formulation of documentary discourse is uniform, beginning with the language preference. What then are some of the documentary facts? Here are some: this saying (in Hebrew) or story occurs here (in Hebrew), bears these traits, is used for this larger re-

---

but rather as the product of a 'vast and uninterrupted dialogue' with other texts" (Henry M. Sayre, *The Object of Performance: The American Avant Garde since 1970* [Chicago: The University of Chicago Press, 1989], 23). A current definition, provided by Julia Kristeva as cited by Sayre, (23), holds that "each text situates itself at the junction of many texts of which it is at once the re-reading, the accentuation, the condensation, the displacement, and the profound extension." As part of a larger reading of literature, the theory of intertextuality has brought into question "not only the importance of the author, the audience, and the text as document, but tries to undermine all previous scholarship and the very concept of truth" (Peter Gaeffke, "The State of Scholarship: A Rock in the Tide of Time: Oriental Studies Then and Now," *Academic Questions* [Spring 1990]: 73). Viewing documents as indeterminate as to both boundaries and truth contradicts the premises of the Judaic canonical writings. Green's statement, cited at the beginning of this chapter, certainly affords slight support for the allegations of the intertextualist reading of any rabbinic writing, whether compiling Midrash exegeses or Mishnah exegeses.

dactional and programmatic purpose, (which is stated in Aramaic), makes this distinct point in its context—always implicit, rarely explicit, in the very choice of the Aramaic language. These facts of linguistic taxonomy therefore define the initial context of interpretation.

Part Two

The Logic of Coherent Exposition

Chapter 2

The Problem of the Composite
Character of the Talmud

The intellectual legacy of an ancient people such
as the Jews, who traced their origins back to creation, Abraham, and Sinai by the writing of the
Bavli two millennia or more into antiquity, comprises a rich and complex inheritance. Themes, issues, and ideas handed on through writings out of
times past defined perspectives on the everyday of
immediate affairs. All Judaisms appeal to the Pen-
tateuchal Judaism, and so, by definition, formulate
their systems in response to that initial Judaic system. At any given moment, therefore, the statement of culture which the social order sets forth
assumes the character of a palimpsest, layers upon
layers of words viewed only at the end, from the
top. Facing such an excess of data, how are the authors of a foundation-document that proposes to
set forth in a purposive way the rules for the social
order best to proceed? They will accomplish their
goal if they can convey the sense that their writing
tells people pretty much everything out of that lay-
ered and complex past that they think they need to
know. Part of the authority, even the plausibility,
of their writing will then derive from its comprehensive character.

In the case of the Bavli, as I noted above in con-
sidering Talmudic language, there were four im-

portant sources of fixed, verbally formulated, prior knowledge to be incorporated in a process of selection and re-presentation: Scripture, the Mishnah, other materials in the names of the authorities of the Mishnah, and their immediate predecessors. Their topical program, by their own choice, was dictated by the Mishnah, not only as a completed piece of writing but also as a taxon; hence, alongside the Mishnah were preserved sayings assigned the status of Mishnah teachings. They of course acknowledged the priority of the written Torah, Scripture. Critical to the intellectual foundations of the social order as they portrayed them was the compelling power of reason, embodied in the sage—that is, in themselves and in the chain of prior sages whose sayings and arguments were preserved and recapitulated. At any given point, then, the authors of the Bavli undertook a vast labor of recension, recapitulation, re-presentation (and not seldom, mere regurgitation). How to say all that on a single page?

I formulate the problem in the framework of not the technology of thought and the reproduction of thought in writing, but of culture and the transmission of its main points. Since the Talmud preserves and presents the Judaic statement of culture, quite naturally, its framers faced the task of holding together a rich, received heritage of thought, portrayed in the very languages in which that thought had come down. Accordingly, a document in two languages, the Bavli also draws together passages from received, authoritative writings, Scripture, the Mishnah, the Tosefta, and related documents.

That fact on its own imparts to the writing a composite character. The resort to two languages formed one medium for sorting things out, holding them apart but also bringing them into relationship. But that formal means for cogent thought and expression in the writing of a statement of the social order hardly sufficed.

For a second and more pressing problem derived from that same excess of intellectual inheritance. It was the task of holding together and setting forth not only a proposition, but also what, within the substantial received tradition, pertained to it: the established facts. At any given point a substantial corpus of relevant information, subordinate but pertinent discussion, demanded a place. The task of formulating in words, within a single enormous document, the perspectives of a society that originated, in its own view, at Sinai required a means for representing, where necessary, everything known out of the past that related to a specific point in the present. In an earlier context, I asked, Can there be a kind of writing that, in its syntax and grammar, in its use of inherited writing, and in its re-formation and re-presentation of the raw materials of culture, conveys public policy and common causes in not only what is said but how it is said? That same question draws us onward to the problem of how, in a single, sustained treatment of a given topic or proposition, the inherited and available facts of the matter can be joined together in a purposive way. Since the intellectual ambition of our authors required them not only to dictate results but also to display reasoning, argument, and evidence, what formal means served to reproduce the result: everything one needs to know, but nothing one does not need to know, to grasp the point that an author wishes to make?

The answer was found in the formulation, out of well-crafted compositions, of purposeful composites. These composites draw upon already completed writings, where the facts presented in, or the propositions demonstrated by, compositions were required for the larger purpose of the compositor. The compositor of the whole then would arrange the components drawn from ready-made writings in such a way that they filled out his picture of his topic and contributed to the demonstration he wished to accomplish. The result, in writing, preserved that palimpsest quality which the ancient culture presented in the social order: layer upon layer of received tradition, all held together in a single, acutely contemporary formulation, at the present hour. Nothing required out of the past for the purposes of the present was lacking; nothing would be omitted. But neither would anything be preserved for its own sake, as an act of antiquarian piety, for example. Everything found its place within that large composite, in writing, that formed the counterpart to the complex but entirely cogent culture, in attitude and in action alike, that animated the society beyond the book.

Rules of composition of already completed, diverse writing into composites ubiquitously governed the writing down of thought—response to the Mishnah and its norms, to Scripture and its theology—just as much as the rules of linguistic

taxonomy governed in the formulation of that remarkably cogent and coherent writing, the Talmud
of Babylonia. An analysis of the rules of composition that govern in the compilation of the Talmud
of Babylonia must commence within the context of
all canonical writings of the Judaism of the dual
Torah that have reached us from the formative age,
that is, the first seven centuries of the common era.
All of these documents have in common two types
of writing: writing formed for the purpose of
compiling the document, and writing formed for a
purpose other than the documentary one. Distin-
guishing these two kinds of writings and showing
the relationships between the latter and the former
define the problematic of all documents, since
knowing what is original to the compilers of a piece
of writing as distinct from compositions upon
which they have drawn in making their compilation defines the question to be addressed to any
work of compilation, hence its literary problematic.

Rabbinic documents draw upon a fund of completed compositions of thought, compositions that
have taken shape without attention to the needs of
the compilers of those documents. At the same
time these same documents also draw upon materials that have been composed with the requirements of the respective documents in mind. We
understand the character of the Bavli's principal
unit of completed discourse as a composite only
when we fully grasp the types of writing a given
passage holds together.

Within the distinction between writing that
serves a redactional purpose and writing that does

not, four types of completed compositions of thought find a place in rabbinic documents.[1] Each type may be distinguished from the others by appeal to a single criterion of differentiation, that is to say, to traits of precisely the same sort. The indicative traits in particular concern the relationship to the redactional purpose of a piece of writing, viewed overall.

(1) Some writings in a given compilation clearly serve the redactional program of the framers of the document in which those writings occur. The Mishnah is one striking example of a piece of writing that has been formulated in the process of redaction, or, to put it differently, that has been written by those responsible for the final compilation, with only limited evidence of the utilization of writings prepared earlier and for a different kind of document from the one in which they now take their place.

(2) Some writings in a given compilation serve the redactional program not of the document in which they occur, but of some other document, now in our hands. There is no material difference, as to the taxonomy of the writing of the classics in Judaism, between the first and second types; it is a problem of transmission of documents, not their formation. Where authors or compilers of a given document made use of some other document, e.g., Scripture or the Mishnah, they ordinarily give a

---

1. Here I review the argument of my *Making the Classics in Judaism: The Three Stages of Literary Formation* (Atlanta: Scholars Press for Brown Judaic Studies, 1990).

signal that that other document is cited, e.g., "as it is written" or " . . . said," for Scripture, and, "as we have learned as a Tannaite statement" (TNN), for the Mishnah. It is exceedingly rare that a document will fail to insert an explicit mark that another piece of writing is cited.

(3) Some writings in a given compilation serve not the purposes of the document in which they occur but rather a redactional program of a document, or even of a type of document, that we do not now have but can readily envision. In this category we find the possibility of imagining compilations that we do not have, but that could have existed but did not survive; or that could have existed and were then recast into the kinds of writings that people clearly preferred (later on) to produce. Numerous examples of writings clearly have been redacted in accord with a program and plan other than those of any document now in our hands.[2] Stories about sages were told and recorded, but not compiled into complete books, e.g., hagiographies about given authorities. The criterion here is not subjective. We can easily demonstrate that materials of a given type, capable of sustaining a large-scale compilation, were available; but no such compilation was made, so far as extant sources suggest or attest.

(4) Some writings now found in a given compilation stand autonomous of any redactional pro-

---

2. See the many examples in my *Making the Classics in Judaism*. In *Why No Gospels in Talmudic Judaism?*, I was able to point out one kind of book that we could have received but were not given.

gram we have in an existing compilation and of any we can even imagine on the foundations of said writings.

The first of those four kinds of completed units of thought (pericopes), as a matter of hypothesis, fall into the final stage of literary formation. That is to say, at the stage at which an authorship has reached the conclusion that it wishes to compile a document of a given character, that authorship will have made up pieces of writing that serve the purposes of the document it wishes to compile. The second through fourth kinds of completed units of thought come earlier than this writing in the process of the formation of the classics of Judaism represented by the compilation in which this writing now finds its place.

My analytical taxonomy of the writings now collected in various compilations points to three stages in the formation of the classics of Judaism. It also suggests that writing went on outside the framework of the editing of documents, and also within the limits of the formation and framing of documents. Since the framers of a sustained and continuous discussion in the pages of the Bavli drew upon writings of diverse points of origin and classification, one principal task derived from the forming from discrete parts a cogent whole. This they did through the making of composites. The logic of coherence which governed the formation of a composite then requires analysis: just how did the authors put things together as they did, why this way, not that way, and what (if anything) do we learn from the way they did their work about their judgment of the social world beyond?

The problem of the analysis of the Talmud of Babylonia in particular begins with two facts. The first is that the document draws heavily upon diverse types of writings, as I have just now explained. Consequently, at every point we deal with a composite, but at only some points, with a cogent composition, beginning, middle, and end. The second is that the palimpsestic culture had produced no ready solution to the problem of the literary representation of the layers of culture. What I mean is very simple. As writers, the Talmud's authors could not call upon the resources available nowadays for the provision of important, but ancillary information. That is to say, if we in the present age wish to present valuable facts which our argument requires, facts that are necessary for the argument but not sufficient to warrant a position in the exposition and argument at hand, we resort to footnotes. There we fill in the factual gaps and so inform our readers of things they need to know—but not within the rush of exposition and argument.

Further, if we have a considerable disquisition that is generally pertinent to our purpose, but either too long or simply tangential and so not to be located on the page of our argument, we relegate that disquisition to an appendix. These two media for the visual selection of the main point and the subordination of required information or (merely) relevant discussion clear our page and open the way to a sustained and cogent discussion. Not only so, but we are educated to expect that a well-crafted essay will expound everything that is required, point by point in proper time and place — but nothing that is not required. When, therefore, we come to the pages of the Talmud of Babylonia, we find ourselves puzzled by one of the document's paramount traits.

Specifically, the Bavli gives us the impression of having been written by authors in their dotage, who forget what they were talking about, writers unable to focus upon the main point. The reason is that, in the course of a given large-scale composite, we identify a variety of missteps, cases of confusion. An argument aimed at clarifying point A may mention, tangentially, fact X. But then fact X will take over and dictate what comes next, and even what follows. Point A may be lost, only to resurface a page or a folio later. That fact has led many to conclude reasonably that the Talmud meanders, talks about this, that, the other thing, generates confusion and not clarity, lacks purpose and program. So the document seems to many of those who know it most intimately to be a compilation of this and that — a source of information, not argument; a collection of pieces of information, not a purposive essay. Not only so, but the way in which the document is represented — with slight punctuation, in long columns of undifferentiated words — underlines the confused and undifferentiated character of the writing.

What I have claimed in behalf of the document — its cogency not only in detail but in general, its power to set forth not only information but compelling and well-argued propositions — therefore contradicts the acknowledged fact that the writers seem unable to keep straight a single line of argument. And, as a matter of fact, whether or not the original authors wrote out the document or had it memorized (and I think it was the former medium that they used), the aesthetic character of the writing hardly sustains my depiction of the document. Some writings in antiquity can sustain the undifferentiated and unpunctuated column of letters, at best broken up into words. The Mishnah, for example, is highly patterned, with the result that knowledge of the mnemonics of the document by itself instructs us on beginnings, middles, and endings. The way in which the writing is done—matched numbers of syllables for example, recurrent patterns of wordings—instructs the reader on how the document holds together. But that is hardly the case with the Bavli, which is not mnemonically sculptured, as readers of chapter 1, above, will have noticed.

Facing the problem of coherently and cogently representing the layers of a palimpsestic culture, the Bavli's writers appear to have failed to meet the challenge. True, they succeeded in supplying a vast amount of information—authoritative rules, principles of argument, examples of practical logic and applied reason. But a glance at any given page leaves the impression that the success was in detail, but the failure, comprehensive. For people unable to keep track of their argument, constantly veering off hither and yon may say memorable things, but they do not win sustained attention. Therefore they may provide useful information but they are not going to shape perspective or impart to culture a single character, or to politics a cogent structure or compelling purpose. Indeed, incompetence at redaction (composing long and sustained arguments of cogency and integrity) in the end leaves as trivial and unpersuasive any ambitious effort at saying everything all at once and all in one place. And that judgment on the success of the Talmud enjoys substantial support in the character of the writing. But it is contradicted, as I have argued throughout these pages, by the astonishing success of the Talmud in compelling assent through persuasion, and in demonstrating how things must be and be done through ineluctable example.

The upshot is that those who received the document understood something that we do not. They could find sustained argument where we see only chaotic arrangements of discrete arguments. They grasped the thrust and purpose of discourse, where we perceive only anecdote and argument by example. So they knew something that we have now to find out, which is how our authors have framed a well-crafted discussion without the advantage of footnotes and appendices for bearing the burden of relevant, but intrusive information. And it was something not to be learned within the norms of the presentation of writing that we derive from our masters of the West, Plato and Aristotle for example, both of whom can be read, sentence by sentence, paragraph by paragraph, beginning to end, in ways in which the Bavli in no manner of conception can be read. One impression we rarely derive from a reading of a dialogue of Plato or a treatise of Aristotle is that the great philosopher has forgotten what he said three sentences ago—I mean, not the point, but the very topic! But even the sample of the Bavli already presented in part 1 is likely to have given the reader the impression that its authors possessed only a rather feeble grasp of the requirements of cogent argument and sustained, systematic presentation of ideas.

In order to show how we have to understand the Bavli in order to grasp its authors' success both in holding together in a single statement a vast heritage of information and in portraying within the technical limitations of their "page"—that is, vast tracts of undifferentiated and unpunctuated words (which can even have been memorized!)—let me give a page of the Talmud in two ways. First, I shall present it precisely as a vast undifferentiated tract, and then I shall show, by a simple process of indentation, the components of the whole that were primary, and those that, in our technology, we are able to designate as footnotes or even appendices. In this way we shall see how a decent effort at following not only the outcome, but the problem of writing which our authors addressed yields considerable respect for the order and structure of their writing. Then my claim that they have ordered and structured a vast amount of received information, doing so in such a way as to provide a full account of everything one needed to know to form and sustain that orderly society, resting on deep foundations of history and revelation, will be validated. For, as I have insisted, the way in which the document expresses its ideas bears the judgment upon society and culture which the authors wished to set forth: the medium not only bears, but itself replicates, the message.

To show that it is a cogent message, I have now to address that issue of the run-on character of discourse that correctly troubles students of the document. Anyone who has "learned" more than ten consecutive lines at a single sitting will have faced this problem of the unruly style of making up composites. Now, therefore, the reader too must undergo the experience of an encounter with an undifferentiated text, merely translated fairly literally, but in no way re-presented within the extant technology by which we organize information in a purposeful manner. In what follows, I first present, without comment, a sizable abstract, marking each sentence off from the others only for the purpose of allowing the reader some sort of minimal access to what is said. I do not differentiate between Hebrew and Aramaic, and I do not include any signals on how a given sentence relates to what has gone before or to what is to follow. So I omit the signals that I have devised to ease the reader's progress through the document, that is, not highlighting what the intended audience automatically will have grasped from shifts in language and other signals, articulated or implicit, in the flow of language. Then, immediately afterward, I represent the entire passage, this time showing it as a differentiated set of citations and quotations from various sources (now, the passages of the Mishnah and Tosefta will be in boldface type), differentiating the two languages, and so drawing upon the signals that language choice delivers, and also displaying in indentation—further and further to the right hand column, as an item glosses a gloss, or provides an appendix to a gloss, or footnotes a footnote—what I conceive to be the secondary or subordinated discussions. The discussion will then show how in presenting a vast corpus of material, and in fully providing the apparatus of information, not only the main points of proposition, evidence, and argument, the framers have followed a few simple rules, which a sensitive reader will have grasped after only minimal study. Here is the whole, differentiated only by commas and periods and quotation marks, single and double, as required, sentence by sentence:

> **[Bavli Abodah Zarah 2A]** For three days before the festivals of gentiles it is forbidden to do business with them, to lend anything to them or to borrow anything from them, to lend money to them or to borrow money from them, to repay them or to be repaid by them. R. Judah says, "They accept repayment from them, because it is distressing to him." They said to him, "Even though it is distressing to him now, he will be happy about it later." Rab and Samuel [in dealing with the reading of the key-word of the Mishnah, translated festival, the letters of which are 'aleph daled, rather than 'ayin daled, which means, calamity]: one repeated the formulation of the Mishnah as, "their festivals." And the other repeated the formulation of the Mishnah as "their

calamities." The one who repeated the
formulation of the Mishnah as "their festivals"
made no mistake, and the one who repeated
the formulation of the Mishnah as "their
calamities" made no mistake. For it is written,
"For the day of their calamity is at hand" (Dt.
32:15). The one who repeated the formulation
of the Mishnah as "their festivals" made no
mistake, for it is written, "Let them bring their
testimonies that they may be justified" (Is.
43:9). And as to the position of him who
repeats the formulation of the Mishnah as
"their festivals," on what account does he not
repeat the formulation of the Mishnah to yield,
"their calamities"? He will say to you,
" 'Calamity' is preferable [as the word choice
when speaking of idolatry]." And as to the
position of him who repeats the formulation of
the Mishnah as "their calamities," on what
account does he not repeat the formulation of
the Mishnah to yield "their festivals"? He will
say to you, "What causes the calamity that
befalls them if not their testimony, so
testimony is preferable!" And as to the verse,
"Let them bring their testimonies that they
may be justified" (Is. 43:9), is this written with
reference to gentiles? Lo, it is written in regard
to Israel. For said R. Joshua b. Levi, "All of the
religious duties that Israelites carry out in this
world come and give testimony in their behalf
in the world to come: 'Let them bring their
witnesses that they may be justified' (Is. 43:9),
that is, Israel; 'and let them hear and say, It is

truth' (Is. 43:9)—this refers to gentiles."

Rather, said R. Huna b. R. Joshua, "He who formulates the Mishnah to refer to their calamities derives the reading from this verse: 'They that fashion a graven image are all of them vanity, and their delectable things shall not profit, and their own witnesses see not nor know' (Is. 44:9)." As to the exposition [of the verse, "They that fashion a graven image are all of them vanity, and their delectable things shall not profit, and their own witnesses see not nor know" (Is. 44:9)]: "In the age to come the Holy One, blessed be he, will bring a scroll of the Torah and hold it in his bosom and say, 'Let him who has kept himself busy with it come and take his reward.' Then all the gentiles will crowd together: 'All of the nations are gathered together' (Is. 43:9). The Holy One, blessed be he, will say to them, 'Do not crowd together before me in a mob. But let each nation enter together with [2B] its scribes, 'and let the peoples be gathered together' (Is. 43:9), and the word 'people' means 'kingdom': 'and one kingdom shall be stronger than the other' (Gen. 25:23)." But can there be a mob scene before the Holy One, blessed be he? Rather, it is so that from their perspective they do not form a mob, so that they will be able to hear what he says to them. "The kingdom of Rome comes in first." How come? Because they are the most important. How do we know on the basis of Scripture they are the most important? Because it is written, "And he

shall devour the whole earth and shall tread it
down and break it into pieces" (Gen. 25:23),
and said R. Yohanan, "This Rome is
answerable, for its definition [of matters] has
gone forth to the entire world [Mishcon: 'this
refers to Rome, whose power is known to the
whole world']." And how do we know that
the one who is most important comes in first?
It is in accord with that which R. Hisda said.
For said R. Hisda, "When the king and the
community [await judgment], the king enters
in first for judgment: 'That he maintain the
case of his servant [Solomon] and [then] the
cause of his people Israel' (1 Kgs. 8:59)." And
how come? If you wish, I shall say it is not
appropriate to keep the king sitting outside.
And if you wish, I shall say that [the king is
allowed to plea his case] before the anger of
the Holy One is aroused." "The Holy One,
blessed be he, will say to them, 'How have
you defined your chief occupation?' They will
say before him, 'Lord of the world, a vast
number of marketplaces have we set up, a vast
number of bathhouses have we made, a vast
amount of silver and gold have we
accumulated. And all of these things we have
done only in behalf of Israel, so that they may
define as their chief occupation the study of
the Torah.' The Holy One, blessed be he, will
say to them, 'You complete idiots! Whatever
you have done has been for your own
convenience. You have set up a vast number of
marketplaces to be sure, but that was so as to

set up whorehouses in them. The bathhouses
were for your own pleasure. Silver and gold
belong to me anyhow: "Mine is the silver and
mine is the gold, says the Lord of hosts" (Hag.
2:8). Are there any among you who have been
telling of "this," and "this" is only the Torah:
"And this is the Torah that Moses set before
the children of Israel" (Dt. 4:44).' So they will
make their exit, humiliated. When the
kingdom of Rome has made its exit, the
kingdom of Persia enters afterward." How
come? Because they are second in importance.
And how do we know it on the basis of
Scripture? Because it is written, "And behold,
another beast, a second, like a bear" (Dan.
7:5), and in this connection R. Joseph repeated
as a Tannaite formulation, "This refers to the
Persians, who eat and drink like a bear, are
obese like a bear, are shaggy like a bear, and
are restless like a bear." The Holy One,
blessed be he, will say to them, 'How have
you defined your chief occuaption?' he will say
before him, 'Lord of the world, We have
thrown up a vast number of bridges, we have
conquered a vast number of towns, we have
made a vast number of wars, and all of them
we did only for Israel, so that they may define
as their chief occupation the study of the
Torah.' The Holy One, blessed be he, will say
to them, 'Whatever you have done has been
for your own convenience. You have thrown
up a vast number of bridges, to collect tolls,
you have conquered a vast number of towns,

to collect the corvée, and, as to making a vast
number of wars, I am the one who makes
wars: "The Lord is a man of war" (Ex. 19:17).
Are there any among you who have been
telling of "this," and "this" is only the Torah:
"And this is the Torah that Moses set before
the children of Israel" (Dt. 4:44).' So they will
make their exit, humiliated. But if the kingdom
of Persia has seen that such a claim issued by
the kingdom of Rome did no good
whatsoever, how come they go in at all?" They
will say to themselves, "These are the ones
who destroyed the house of the sanctuary, but
we are the ones who built it." And so it will
go with each and every nation." But if each
one of them has seen that such a claim issued
by the others did no good whatsoever, how
come they go in at all? They will say to
themselves, "Those two subjugated Israel, but
we never subjugated Israel." And how come
the two conquering nations are singled out as
important and the others are not? It is because
the rule of these will continue until the
Messiah comes. "They will say to him, 'Lord
of the world, in point of fact, did you actually
give it to us and we did not accept it?' " But
how can they present such an argument, since
it is written, "The Lord came from Sinai and
rose from Seir to them, he shined forth from
Mount Paran" (Dt. 33:2), and further, "God
comes from Teman" (Hab. 3:3). Now what in
the world did he want in Seir, and what was
he looking for in Paran? Said R. Yohanan,

"This teaches that the Holy One, blessed be
he, made the rounds of each and every nation
and language and none accepted it, until he
came to Israel, and they accepted it." Rather,
this is what they say, "Did we accept it but
then not carry it out?" But to this the rejoinder
must be, "Why did you not accept it anyhow!"
Rather, "this is what they say before him,
'Lord of the world, Did you hold a mountain
over us like a cask and then we refused to
accept it as you did to Israel, as it is written,
"And they stood beneath the mountain" (Ex.
19:17).' " And [in connection with the verse,
"And they stood beneath the mountain" (Ex.
19:17),] said R. Dimi bar Hama, "This teaches
that the Holy One, blessed be he, held the
mountain over Israel like a cask and said to
them, 'If you accept the Torah, well and good,
and if not, then there is where your grave will
be.' " "Then the Holy One, blessed be he, will
say to them, 'Let us make known what
happened first: "Let them announce to us
former things" (Is. 43:9). As to the seven
religious duties that you did accept, where
have you actually carried them out?' " And
how do we know on the basis of Scripture that
they did not carry them out? R. Joseph
formulated as a Tannaite statement, " 'He
stands and shakes the earth, he sees and
makes the nations tremble' (Hab. 3:6): what
did he see? He saw the seven religious duties
that the children of Noah accepted upon
themselves as obligations but never actually

carried them out. Since they did not carry out
those obligations, he went and remitted their
obligation." But then they benefited—so it
pays to sin! Said Mar b. Rabina, **[3A]** "What
this really proves is that even they who carry
out those religious duties, they get no reward
on that account." And they don't, do they?
But has it not been taught on Tannaite
authority: R. Meir would say, "How on the
basis of Scripture do we know that, even if it
is a gentile, if he goes and takes up the study
of the Torah as his occupation, he is equivalent
to the high priest? Scripture states, 'You shall
therefore keep my statutes and my ordinances,
which, if a human being does them, one shall
gain life through them' (Lev. 18:5). What is
written is not 'priests' or 'Levites' or
'Israelites,' but rather, 'a human being.' So you
have learned the fact that, even if it is a
gentile, if he goes and takes up the study of
the Torah as his occupation, he is equivalent to
the high priest." Rather, what you learn from
this is that they will not receive that reward
that is coming to those who are commanded to
do them and who carry them out, but rather,
the reward that they receive will be like that
coming to the one who is not commanded to
do them and who carries them out anyhow.
For said R. Hanina, "Greater is the one who is
commanded and who carries out the religious
obligations than the one who is not
commanded but nonetheless carries out
religious obligations." "This is what the

gentiles say before him, 'Lord of the world,
Israel, who accepted it—where in the world
have they actually carried it out?' The Holy
One, blessed be he, will say to them, 'I shall
bear witness concerning them, that they have
carried out the whole of the Torah!' They will
say before him, 'Lord of the world, is there a
father who is permitted to give testimony
concerning his son? For it is written, "Israel is
my son, my first born" (Ex. 4:22).' The Holy
One, blessed be he, will say to them, 'The
heaven and the earth will give testimony in
their behalf that they have carried out the
entirety of the Torah.' They will say before
him, 'Lord of the world, The heaven and earth
have a selfish interest in the testimony that
they give: "If not for my covenant with day
and with night, I should not have appointed
the ordinances of heaven and earth" (Jer.
33:25).' " For said R. Simeon b. Laqish, "What
is the meaning of the verse of Scripture, 'And
there was evening, and there was morning,
the sixth day' (Gen. 1:31)? This teaches that
the Holy One, blessed be he, made a
stipulation with all of the works of creation,
saying to them, 'If Israel accepts my Torah,
well and good, but if not, I shall return you to
chaos and void.' That is in line with what is
written: 'You did cause sentence to be heard
from heaven, the earth trembled and was still'
(Ps. 76:9). If 'trembling' then where is the
stillness, and if stillness, then where is the
trembling? Rather, to begin with, trembling,

but at the end, stillness. The Holy One, blessed be he, will say to them, 'Some of them may well come and give testimony concerning Israel that they have observed the entirety of the Torah. Let Nimrod come and give testimony in behalf of Abraham that he never worshiped idols. Let Laban come and give testimony in behalf of Jacob, that he never was suspect of thievery. Let the wife of Potiphar come and give testimony in behalf of Joseph, that he was never suspect of "sin." Let Nebuchadnessar come and give testimony in behalf of Hananiah, Mishael, and Azariah, that they never bowed down to the idol. Let Darius come and give testimony in behalf of Daniel, that he did not neglect even the optional prayers. Let Bildad the Shuhite and Zophar the Naamatite and Eliphaz the Temanite and Elihu son of Barachel the Buzite come and testify in behalf of Israel that they have observed the entirety of the Torah: "Let the nations bring their own witnesses, that they may be justified" (Is. 43:9).' They will say to him, 'Then give it to us to begin with, and let us carry it out.' The Holy One, blessed be he, will say to them, 'World-class idiots! He who took the trouble to prepare on the eve of the Sabbath [Friday] will eat on the Sabbath, but he who took no trouble on the eve of the Sabbath—what in the world is he going to eat on the Sabbath! Still, [I'll give you another chance.] I have a rather simple religious duty, which is called "the tabernacle." Go and do that one.' '' But can you say any such thing? Lo, R. Joshua b. Levi has said, "What is the meaning of the verse of Scripture, 'The ordinances that I command you this day to do them' (Dt. 7:11)? Today is the day to do them, but not tomorrow; they are not to be done tomorrow; today is the day to do them, but not the day on which to receive a reward for doing them. Rather, it is that the Holy One, blessed be he, does not exercise tyranny over his creatures. And why does he refer to it as a simple religious duty? Because it does not involve enormous expense [to carry out that religious duty]. Forthwith every one of them will take up the task and go and make a tabernacle on his roof. But then the Holy, One, blessed be he, will come and make the sun blaze over them as at the sumer solstice, and every one of them will knock down his tabernacle and go his way: 'Let us break their bands asunder and cast away their cords from us' (Ps. 23:3).'' But lo, you have just said, "it is that the Holy One, blessed be he, does not exercise tyranny over his creatures"! (It is because the Israelites too—sometimes **[3B]** the summer solstice goes on to the Festival of Tabernacles, and therefore they are bothered by the heat! But has not Raba stated, "One who is bothered [by the heat] is exempt from the obligation of dwelling in the tabernacle"? Granting that one may be exempt from the duty, is he going to go and tear the thing down? "Then the Holy One, blessed be he, goes into session and laughs at them: 'He who sits in heaven laughs' (Ps. 2:4)." Said R. Isaac, "Laughter before the Holy One, blessed be he, takes place only on that day alone." There are those who repeat as a Tannaite version this statement of R. Isaac in respect to that which has been taught on Tannaite authority: R. Yosé says, "In the coming age gentiles will come and convert." But will they be accepted? Has it not been taught on Tannaite authority: Converts will not be accepted in the days of the Messiah, just as they did not accept proselytes either in the time of David or in the time of Solomon? Rather, "they will make themselves converts, and they will put on phylacteries on their heads and arms and fringes on their garments and a mezuzah on their doors. But when they witness the war of Gog and Magog, he will say to them, 'How come you have come?' They will say, ' "Against the Lord and against his Messiah." ' For so it is said, 'Why are the nations in an uproar and why do the peoples mutter in vain' (Ps. 2:1). Then each one of them will rid himself of his religious duty and go his way: 'Let us break their bands asunder' (Ps. 2:3). Then the Holy One, blessed be he, goes into session and laughs at them: 'He who sits in heaven laughs' (Ps. 2:4)." Said R. Isaac, "Laughter before the Holy One, blessed be he, takes place only on that day alone." But is this really so? And has not R. Judah said Rab said, "The day is made up of twelve hours. In the first three the Holy One, blessed be he, goes into session and engages in study of the Torah; in the second he goes into session and judges the entire world. When he realizes that the world is liable to annihilation, he arises from the throne of justice and takes up a seat on the throne of mercy. In the third period he goes into session and nourishes the whole world from the horned buffalo to the brood of vermin. During the fourth quarter he laughs [and plays] with leviathan: 'There is leviathan, whom you have formed to play with' (Ps. 104:26)." [This proves that God does laugh more than on that one day alone.] Said R. Nahman bar Isaac, "With his creatures he laughs [everyday], but at his creatures he laughs only on that day alone."

That is what the page without markings other than periods and quotation marks yields. Anyone with the patience to read the entire passage will by now have found utterly implausible my allegation that the page is well-crafted, coherent, and cogent. And even were I to paragraph the column of words, it would make little difference to that judgment.

The movement from the presentation of every-thing in a single block to the representation of the differentiated units of thought, from the smallest whole unit of intelligible statement to the largest complete and exhaustive composite, shows what I have had to do in order to begin the kind of work I wished to accomplish. Specifically, readers will now see very graphically why I found it necessary to retranslate all canonical writings of the Judaism of the dual Torah that already had been presented in English, as well as to translate for the first time those many documents that were not in English when I started my project. It goes without saying that no Hebrew printing of the Talmud has ever made possible any sort of large-scale analytical work at all. Not only so, but I do not believe that any Hebrew edition, e.g., a critical text, at which Israeli colleagues think they excel, will ever attend to that minimum task. Not only so, but—perhaps it was deemed more "authentic" because "traditional"—every translation into various European languages also has failed to provide even the most minimal sigla, e.g., indications of the smallest whole units of thought, sentences, paragraphs, completed expositions of a single idea, components of larger presentations of propositions, and the like—nothing.

No wonder the Bavli (among all writings) is (mis)represented as utterly confused, a hodge-podge of this and that, when, in fact, it is an orderly and well-disciplined construction. The whole of rabbinic literature has had to be retranslated in such a way as to indicate the individual components of a composition, e.g., sentences, paragraphs, chapters, or completed whole presentations of propositions. I have accomplished most of that task, out of an interest in not philology, let alone text criticism, but history of religion. In the present context I ask about the Bavli as a statement of a system: Can the document be read to attest to an orderly and cogent worldview and way of life addressed to a social entity called (an) Israel? My task here is not to propose an alternative to some other claim concerning the systematic character of the Bavli and how that system of thought and expression is to be described. Rather, it is to demonstrate that the document exhibits a systematic and orderly character in the face of the widely held, but ignorant, view to the contrary.

Without further ado, I now reconsider the entire passage, now differentiating sources by different typefaces, and text from footnotes and appendices by indenting (and doubly and triply indenting) the latter. The reader is referred to the account of my reference system, given in chapter 1, note 6, for further explanation of the sigla. In this way we see precisely what is in play on the page; my comments then will explain what the authors have done to give us everything they thought we had to know. We see that they followed a few simple rules, which we can discern and which guide us in reading their writing.

1:1

A. [2A] **Before the festivals of gentiles for three days it is forbidden to do business with them.**

B. **(1) to lend anything to them or to borrow anything from them.**

C. **(2) to lend money to them or to borrow money from them.**

D. **(3) to repay them or to be repaid by them.**

E. **R. Judah says, "They accept repayment from them, because it is distressing to him."**

F. **They said to him, "Even though it is distressing to him now, he will be happy about it later."**

Mishnah 1:1.I.1 A. [2A] Rab and Samuel [in dealing with the reading of the key-word of the Mishnah, translated festival, the letters of which are 'aleph daled, rather than 'ayin daled, which means, calamity]:

B. *one repeated the formulation of the Mishnah as, "their festivals."*

C. *And the other repeated the formulation of the Mishnah as "their calamities."*

D. *The one who repeated the formulation of the Mishnah as "their festivals" made no mistake, and the one who repeated the formulation of the Mishnah as "their calamities" made no mistake.*

E. *For it is written,* "For the day of their calamity is at hand" (Dt. 32:15).

F. *The one who repeated the formulation of the Mishnah as "their festivals" made no mistake, for it is written,* "Let them bring their testimonies that they may be justified" (Is. 43:9).

G. *And as to the position of him who repeats the formulation of the Mishnah as "their festivals," on what account does he not repeat the formulation of the Mishnah to yield, "their calamities"?*

H. *He will say to you, "* 'Calamity' is preferable [as the word choice when speaking of idolatry]."

I. *And as to the position of him who repeats the formulation of the Mishnah as "their calamities," on what account does he not repeat the formulation of the Mishnah to yield "their festivals"?*

J. *He will say to you, "What causes the calamity that befalls them if not their testimony, so testimony is preferable!"*

K. *And as to the verse,* "Let them bring their testimonies that they may be justified" (Is. 43:9), *is this written with reference to gentiles? Lo, it is written in regard to Israel.*

L. For said R. Joshua b. Levi, "All of the religious duties that Israelites carry out in this world come and give testimony in their behalf in the world to come: 'Let them bring their witnesses that they may be justified' (Is. 43:9), that is, Israel; 'and let them hear and say, It is truth' (Is. 43:9)—this refers to gentiles."

M. Rather, said R. Huna b. R. Joshua, "He who formulates the Mishnah to refer to their calamities derives the reading from this verse: 'They that fashion a graven image are all of them vanity, and their delectable things shall not profit, and their own witnesses see not nor know' (Is. 44:9)."

The foregoing, we see clearly, presents a beautifully balanced dispute form, and the form is used to provide a medium for presenting Mishnah text criticism: how are we to read the text of the paragraph before us? That classification presents no problems. We must now enter a much more difficult question, because I maintain that, along with the classification of I.1, everything that is attached to I.1 in a continuous and ongoing manner goes along as a single composite, the whole put together in its own terms, but is then utilized by the framer of the Talmud before us—folios 2A–5B—as a continuous (if in our perspective rather run-on) statement. It is obviously a composite. But I classify the entire composite all together and all at once, because it is more than a composite: it also is a composition. And the reason I see it as a coherent and cogent composition is that every item fits together with its predecessor and leads us without interruption to its successor, from the starting lines of I.1 to the concluding ones of I.32.

No. 1 has referred us to gentile idolatry and Israelite loyalty to the religious duties assigned to them by God. We now have a long exposition of the theme of gentile idolatry and perfidy. Everything that follows in I.2 serves as a play on the theme of I.1 L–M! The unity of the whole of I.2 will be readily apparent because of the insets of gloss and expansion, and the further insets of the appendices to the gloss and expansion. We shall now see, through the device of indentations, how much in the expansion of the foregoing in fact serves as gloss, footnote, and appendix; recognizing that fact we see a rather well-crafted and cogent composite, made up of a principal composition— extending to the far left-hand margin—and a variety of subordinated compositions, moving off to the right in progressive indentations. And what we can see, visually, any well-endowed disciple of the document will readily have understood through his or her thoughtful reading of the document: this is primary; that is secondary and subordinate. In ages past the disciples will not have called what I indent "footnotes" or even "appendices." But they also will not have found confusing the glosses and supplements that, all together, give a full and rich account of any subject introduced in the primary discussion.

True, this is not how Plato and Aristotle set out their ideas; but the great philosophers also did not choose as the medium for writing down their ideas a commentary on a received text, in constant dialogue with yet another received text (the Mishnah, Scripture), with persistent attention to a variety of other received data, all to be provided in a complete and purposeful argument on a point of fundamental importance. They simply set forth a complete and purposeful argument in behalf of a proposition; the evidence and argument were recast by the philosophers into the language required for the proposition they wished to argue, whether in dialogue or in dialectical form. The character of the Judaic sages' system—the inheritance of revelation with which they proposed to enter dialogue —called forth a form that, in itself, expressed the character of the nurturing culture beyond.

I.2 A. R. Hanina bar Pappa, and some say, R. Simlai, gave the following exposition [of the verse, "They that fashion a graven image are all of them vanity, and their delectable things shall not profit, and their own witnesses see not nor know" (Is. 44:9)]: "In the age to come the Holy One, blessed be he, will bring a scroll of the Torah and hold it in his bosom and say, 'Let him who has kept himself busy with it come and take his reward.' Then all the gentiles will crowd together: 'All of the nations are gathered together' (Is. 43:9). The Holy One, blessed be he, will say to them, 'Do not crowd together before me in a mob. But let each nation enter together with [2B] its scribes, 'and let the peoples be gathered together' (Is. 43:9), and the word 'people' means 'kingdom': 'and one kingdom shall be stronger than the other' (Gen. 25:23)."

B. *But can there be a mob scene before the Holy One, blessed be he? Rather, it is so that from their perspective they do not form a mob, so that they will be able to hear what he says to them.*

C. [Resuming the narrative of A:] "The kingdom of Rome comes in first."

D. *How come? Because they are the most important. How do we know on the basis of Scripture they are the most important? Because it is written,* "And he shall devour the whole earth and shall tread it down and break it into pieces" (Gen. 25:23), and said R. Yohanan, "This Rome is answerable, for its definition [of matters] has gone forth to the entire world [Mishcon: 'this refers to Rome, whose power is known to the whole world']."

E. *And how do we know that the one who is most important comes in first? It is in accord with that which R. Hisda said.*

F. For said R. Hisda, "When the king and the community [await judgment], the king enters in first for judgment: 'That he maintain the case of his servant [Solomon] and [then] the cause of his people Israel' (1 Kgs. 8:59)."

G. *And how come? If you wish, I shall say it is not appropriate to keep the king sitting outside. And if you wish, I shall say that [the king is allowed to plea his case] before the anger of the Holy One is aroused.*"

H. [Resuming the narrative of C:] "The Holy One, blessed be he, will say to them, 'How have you defined your chief occupation?'

I. "They will say before him, 'Lord of the world, a vast number of marketplaces have we set up, a vast number of bathhouses have we made, a vast amount of silver and gold have we accumulated. And all of these things we have done only in behalf of Israel, so that they may define as their chief occupation the study of the Torah.'

J. "The Holy One, blessed be he, will say to them, 'You complete idiots! Whatever you have done has been for your own convenience. You have set up a vast number of marketplaces to be sure, but that was so as to set up whorehouses in them. The bathhouses were for your own pleasure. Silver and gold belong to me anyhow: "Mine is the silver and mine is the gold, says the Lord of hosts" (Hag. 2:8). Are there any among you who have been telling of "this," and "this" is only the Torah: "And this is the Torah that Moses set before the children of Israel" (Dt. 4:44).' So they will make their exit, humiliated.

K. "When the kingdom of Rome has made its exit, the kingdom of Persia enters afterward."

L. *How come? Because they are second in importance. And how do we know it on the basis of Scripture? Because it is written,* "And behold, another beast, a second, like a bear" (Dan. 7:5), *and in this connection R. Joseph repeated as a Tannaite formulation,* "This refers to the Persians, who eat and drink like a bear, are obese like a bear, are shaggy like a bear, and are restless like bear."

M. "The Holy One, blessed be he, will say to them, 'How have you defined your chief occupation?'

N. "They will say before him, 'Lord of the world, We have thrown up a vast number of bridges, we have conquered a vast number of towns, we have made a vast number of wars, and all of them we did only for Israel, so that they may define as their chief occupation the study of the Torah.'

O. "The Holy One, blessed be he, will say to them, 'Whatever you have done has been for your own convenience. You have thrown up a vast number of bridges, to collect tolls, you have conquered a vast number of towns, to collect the corvée, and, as to making a vast number of wars, I am the one who makes wars: "The Lord is a man of war" (Ex. 19:17). Are there any among you who have been telling of "this," and "this" is only the Torah:

"And this is the Torah that Moses set before the children of Israel" (Dt. 4:44).' So they will make their exit, humiliated.

P. *But if the kingdom of Persia has seen that such a claim issued by the kingdom of Rome did no good whatsoever, how come they go in at all?*

Q. *They will say to themselves, "These are the ones who destroyed the house of the sanctuary, but we are the ones who built it."*

R. "And so it will go with each and every nation."

S. *But if each one of them has seen that such a claim issued by the others did no good whatsoever, how come they go in at all?*

T. *They will say to themselves, "Those two subjugated Israel, but we never subjugated Israel."*

U. *And how come the two conquering nations are singled out as important and the others are not?*

V. *It is because the rule of these will continue until the Messiah comes.*

W. "They will say to him, 'Lord of the world, in point of fact, did you actually give it to us and we did not accept it?' "

X. *But how can they present such an argument, since it is written, "The Lord came from Sinai and rose from Seir to them, he shined forth from Mount Paran" (Dt. 33:2), and further, "God comes from Teman" (Hab. 3:3). Now what in the world did he want in Seir, and what was he looking for in Paran? Said R. Yohanan, "This teaches that the Holy One, blessed be*

he, made the rounds of each and every
nation and language and none accepted it,
until he came to Israel, and they accepted
it."

Y. *Rather, this is what they say*, "Did we
accept it but then not carry it out?"

Z. *But to this the rejoinder must be*, "Why did
you not accept it anyhow!"

AA. Rather, "this is what they say before him,
'Lord of the world, Did you hold a mountain
over us like a cask and then we refused to
accept it as you did to Israel, as it is written,
"And they stood beneath the mountain" (Ex.
19:17).' "

BB. And [in connection with the verse,
"And they stood beneath the mountain"
(Ex. 19:17),] said R. Dimi bar Hama, "This
teaches that the Holy One, blessed be he,
held the mountain over Israel like a cask and
said to them, 'If you accept the Torah, well
and good, and if not, then there is where
your grave will be.' "

CC. "Then the Holy One, blessed be he, will
say to them, 'Let us make known what
happened first: "Let them announce to us
former things" (Is. 43:9). As to the seven
religious duties that you did accept, where
have you actually carried them out?' "

DD. *And how do we know on the basis of
Scripture that they did not carry them out? R.
Joseph formulated as a Tannaite statement*, " 'He
stands and shakes the earth, he sees and
makes the nations tremble' (Hab. 3:6): what

did he see? He saw the seven religious
duties that the children of Noah accepted
upon themselves as obligations but never
actually carried them out. Since they did not
carry out those obligations, he went and
remitted their obligation."

EE. *But then they benefited—so it pays to sin!*

FF. Said Mar b. Rabina, **[3A]** "What this
really proves is that even they who carry out
those religious duties, they get no reward on
that account."

GG. *And they don't, do they? But has it not
been taught on Tannaite authority:* R. Meir
would say, "How on the basis of Scripture
do we know that, even it if is a gentile, if he
goes and takes up the study of the Torah as
his occupation, he is equivalent to the high
priest? Scripture states, 'You shall therefore
keep my statutes and my ordinances, which,
if a human being does them, one shall gain
life through them' (Lev. 18:5). What is
written is not 'priests' or 'Levites' nor
'Israelites,' but rather, 'a human being.' So
you have learned the fact that, even if it is a
gentile, if he goes and takes up the study of
the Torah as his occupation, he is equivalent
to the high priest."

HH. Rather, what you learn from the [DD]
is that they will not receive that reward that
is coming to those who are commanded to
do them and who carry them out, but
rather, the reward that they receive will be
like that coming to the one who is not

commanded to do them and who carries them out anyhow.

II. For said R. Hanina, "Greater is the one who is commanded and who carries out the religious obligations than the one who is not commanded but nonetheless carries out religious obligations."

JJ. [Reverting to AA:] "This is what the gentiles say before him, 'Lord of the world, Israel, who accepted it—where in the world have they actually carried it out?'

KK. "The Holy One, blessed be he, will say to them, 'I shall bear witness concerning them, that they have carried out the whole of the Torah?'

LL. "They will say before him, 'Lord of the world, is there a father who is permitted to give testimony concerning his son? For it is written, "Israel is my son, my firstborn" (Ex. 4:22).'

MM. "The Holy One, blessed be he, will say to them, 'The heaven and the earth will give testimony in their behalf that they have carried out the entirety of the Torah.'

NN. "They will say before him, "Lord of the world, The heaven and earth have a selfish interest in the testimony that they give: "If not for my covenant with day and with night, I should not have appointed the ordinances of heaven and earth" (Jer. 33:25).' "

OO. *For said R. Simeon b. Laqish, "What is the meaning of the verse of Scripture, 'And there was evening, and there was morning, the* sixth day' (Gen. 1:31)? This teaches that the Holy One, blessed be he, made a stipulation with all of the works of creation, saying to them, 'If Israel accepts my Torah, well and good, but if not, I shall return you to chaos and void.' *That is in line with what is written:* 'You did cause sentence to be heard from heaven, the earth trembled and was still' (Ps. 76:9). If 'trembling' then where is the stillness, and if stillness, then where is the trembling? Rather, to begin with, trembling, but at the end, stillness."

PP. [Reverting to MM–NN]: "The Holy One, blessed be he, will say to them, 'Some of them may well come and give testimony concerning Israel that they have observed the entirety of the Torah. Let Nimrod come and give testimony in behalf of Abraham that he never worshiped idols. Let Laban come and give testimony in behalf of Jacob, that he never was suspect of thievery. Let the wife of Potiphar come and give testimony in behalf of Joseph, that he was never suspect of "sin." Let Nebuchadnessar come and give testimony in behalf of Hananiah, Mishael, and Azariah, that they never bowed down to the idol. Let Darius come and give testimony in behalf of Daniel, that he did not neglect even the optional prayers. Let Bildad the Shuhite and Zophar the Naamatite and Eliphaz the Temanite and Elihu son of Barachel the Buzite come and testify in behalf of Israel that they have observed the entirety of the Torah: "Let the nations bring their own witnesses, that they may be justified" (Is. 43:9).'

PP. "They will say before him, 'Lord of the world, Give it to us to begin with, and let us carry it out.'

QQ. "The Holy One, blessed be he, will say to them, 'World-class idiots! He who took the trouble to prepare on the eve of the Sabbath [Friday] will eat on the Sabbath, but he who took no trouble on the eve of the Sabbath—what in the world is he going to eat on the Sabbath! Still, [I'll give you another chance.] I have a rather simple religious duty, which is called "the tabernacle." Go and do that one.' "

RR. *But can you say any such thing? Lo, R. Joshua b. Levi has said, "What is the meaning of the verse of Scripture, 'The ordinances that I command you this day to do them' (Dt. 7:11)? Today is the day to do them, but not tomorrow; they are not to be done tomorrow; today is the day to do them, but not the day on which to receive a reward for doing them.*

SS. Rather, it is that the Holy One, blessed be he, does not exercise tyranny over his creatures.

TT. *And why does he refer to it as a simple religious duty? Because it does not involve enormous expense [to carry out that religious duty].*

UU. "Forthwith every one of them will take up the task and go and make a tabernacle on his roof. But then the Holy One, blessed be he, will come and make the sun blaze over them, as at the summer solstice, and every one of them will knock down his tabernacle and go his way: 'Let us break their bands asunder and cast away their cords from us' (Ps. 23:3)."

VV. But lo, you have just said, "it is that the Holy One, blessed be he, does not exercise tyranny over his creatures"!

WW. *It is because the Israelites too—sometimes* [3B] *the summer solstice goes on to the Festival of Tabernacles, and therefore they are bothered by the heat!*

XX. But has not Raba stated, "One who is bothered [by the heat] is exempt from the obligation of dwelling in the tabernacle"?

YY. *Granting that one may be exempt from the duty, is he going to go and tear the thing down?*

ZZ. [Continuing from UU:] "Then the Holy One, blessed be he, goes into session and laughs at them: 'He who sits in heaven laughs' (Ps. 2:4)."

AAA. Said R. Isaac, "Laughter before the Holy One, blessed be he, takes place only on that day alone."

BBB. *There are those who repeat as a Tannaite version this statement of R. Isaac in respect to that which has been taught on Tannaite authority:*

CCC. R. Yosé says, "In the coming age gentiles will come and convert."

DDD. *But will they be accepted? Has it not been taught on Tannaite authority:* Converts will not be accepted in the days of the

Messiah, just as they did not accept proselytes either in the time of David or in the time of Solomon?

EEE. Rather, "they will make themselves converts, and they will put on phylacteries on their heads and arms and fringes on their garments and a mezuzah on their doors. But when they witness the war of Gog and Magog, he will say to them, 'How come you have come?' They will say, ' "Against the Lord and against his Messiah." ' For so it is said, 'Why are the nations in an uproar and why do the peoples mutter in vain' (Ps. 2:1). Then each one of them will rid himself of his religious duty and go his way: 'Let us break their bands asunder' (Ps. 2:3). Then the Holy One, blessed be he, goes into session and laughs at them: 'He who sits in heaven laughs' (Ps. 2:4)."

FFF. Said R. Isaac, "Laughter before the Holy One, blessed be he, takes place only on that day alone."

GGG. But is this really so? And has not R. Judah said Rab said, "The day is made up of twelve hours. In the first three the Holy One, blessed be he, goes into session and engages in study of the Torah; in the second he goes into session and judges the entire world. When he realizes that the world is liable to annihilation, he arises from the throne of justice and takes up a seat on

> the throne of mercy. In the third period he goes into session and nourishes the whole world from the horned buffalo to the brood of vermin. During the fourth quarter he laughs [and plays] with leviathan: 'There is leviathan, whom you have formed to play with' (Ps. 104:26)." [This proves that God does laugh more than on that one day alone.]
> HHH. Said R. Nahman bar Isaac, "With his creatures he laughs [everyday], but at his creatures he laughs only on that day alone."

The shift from language to language signals the presence of a sotto voce observation, a gloss, or a footnote. The movement from the main point to an indented composition does not obliterate the character of the whole as a well-crafted composite—a unity from start to finish.

That the whole of the foregoing constitutes a single essay is readily apparent. When the continuing discussion set forth by Hanina bar Pappa or Simlai is interrupted with a gloss, that is readily apparent. To show how that glossing process in our terms would form a footnote, I indent what I conceive to be footnotes. The interesting point comes at BBB, where we have an appendix to AAA. That is to say, the footnote, AAA, completes the foregoing statement, ZZ. Then the additional information is added not to the basic text but to the gloss; it is not filler, the information is valued. But the insertion

clearly adds nothing to the basic text—hence it is
relegated to an appendix, which, in our technical
age, we should simply place at the end of a book.
But then GGG forms a footnote to an appendix,
therefore is indented still further. So much for the
details. The document looks run-on, but proves to
hold together in a cogent way, once we understand
how its authorship has solved a basic problem in
the presentation of what they want to tell us. Now
to explain what is at stake.

Chapter 3

Deconstruction and Social Reconstruction: The Coherence of Community in Literary Representation

Two important propositions now require attention. The first is that in the formation of composites, the framers of a principal component of discourse really did show the connectedness of things, which therefore were demonstrated to make a single point. The second is that, through that demonstration, they represented in literary form the social condition of Israel. The first point is readily established and already has been adumbrated. The second forms the judgment merely of an outsider, an onlooker looking backward at what was achieved. It therefore sustains only the most casual presentation, being less of an interpretation than a guess.

It is perfectly clear, as a matter of fact, that when people addressed compositions and considered how these might be formed into larger composites, more than a single purpose—the purpose dictated by the making of the Talmud—instructed them on what to choose and on how to join this to that. In what follows, I provide a sustained example of how two or more quite distinct principles of conglomeration guided the work, and how only at the end an enormous and quite diverse composite took shape, to be inserted whole into our Talmud. What we shall now see is not merely the presence of footnotes and appendices, but something quite different. It is a massive formation for some purpose quite different from that of forming the Talmud. At the end I shall identify the purpose—that is, the meaning of making connections—for which the bulk of the compositions were formed into a coherent composite. When we grasp the purpose in the following composite, we shall see that the framer of the whole had in mind to make a major statement, which only after the fact served for this enormous thing, this Talmud, that is served by the statement. That observation will then set the stage for my allegation at the end concerning the social bearing of the process of forming a composite: the social reconstruction in merely literary form of a composite and diverse community. So we shall now see that the wandering composite that follows in point of fact addresses a single matter and sets forth a simple statement of public policy.

To clarify what belongs, and what does not belong, to the principal composite—which is not the one that serves as our Talmud—I set off the composite under discussion from what clearly forms the Talmud for our Mishnah paragraph. These materials begin at no. 2.

1:7

A. **They do not sell them (1) bears or (2) lions, or (3) anything which is a public danger.**

B. **They do not build with them (1) a basilica, (2) scaffold, (3) stadium, or (4) judges' tribunal.**

II.1. A. **They do not build with them (1) a basilica, (2) scaffold, (3) stadium, or (4) judges' tribunal:**

B. Said Rabbah b. Bar Hanna said R. Yohanan, "There are three classifications of basilicas: those belonging to gentile kings, those belonging to bathhouses, and those belonging to store houses."

C. Said Raba, "Two of those are permitted, the third forbidden [for Israelite workers to build], and your mnemonic is 'to bind their kings with chains' (Ps. 149:8)."

D. And there are those who say, said Raba, "All of them are permitted [for Israelite workers to build]."

E. *But have we not learned in the Mishnah:* **They do not build with them (1) a basilica, (2) scaffold, (3) stadium, or (4) judges' tribunal?**

F. *Say that that rule applies in particular to* a basilica to which is attached an executioner's scaffold, a stadium, or a judge's tribunal.

II.1 accomplishes the same purpose, of harmonizing opinions. Because of II.1, II.2 is tacked on, and the entire mass of material on rabbis' martyrdoms, already in place, was kept together with the illustration of the tribune and why Israelite workers should not join in building such a thing. To appreciate how a large composite takes shape, let us now review all that follows and identify the compositions that have been joined together and why they serve as they do. As before, I indent what I classify as compositions that serve as footnotes, and I further indent what I deem to be appendices.

2. A. *Our rabbis taught on Tannaite authority:*

B. When R. Eliezer was arrested on charges of minut [being a Christian], they brought him up to the judge's tribunal to be judged. The hegemon said to him, "Should a sage such as yourself get involved in such nonsense as this?"

C. He said to him, "I acknowledge the Judge."

D. The hegemon supposed that he was referring to him, but he referred only to his father who is in heaven. He said to him, "Since I have been accepted by you as an honorable judge, *demos!* You are acquitted."

E. When he got to his household, his disciples came to him to console him, but he did not accept consolation. Said to him R. Aqiba, "My lord, will you let me say something to you from among the things that you have taught me?"

F. He said to him, "Speak."

G. He said to him, "Perhaps some matter pertaining to minut has come into your domain [17A] and given you some sort of satisfaction, and on that account you were arrested?"

H. He said to him, "Aqiba, you remind me! Once I was going in the upper market of

Sepphoris, and I found a certain person, named Jacob of Kefar Sakhnayya, who said to me, 'It is written in your Torah, "You shall not bring the hire of a harlot . . . into the house of the Lord your God" (Dt. 23:19). What is the law as to building with such funds a privy for the high priest?' Now I did not say a thing to him.

I. "So he said to me, 'This is what I have been taught [by Jesus of Nazareth], "For the hire of a harlot has she gathered them, and to the hire of a harlot they shall return" (Prov. 5:8). They have come from a filthy place and to a filthy place they may return.' And that statement gave me a good bit of pleasure, and on that account I was arrested on the charge of being a Christian, so I violated what is written in the Torah: 'Remove your way far from her'—this refers to minut; 'and do not come near to the door of her house' (Prov. 5:8)—this refers to the government."

3. A. There are those who refer "Remove your way far from her," to Christianity and to the ruling power, and the part of the verse, "and do not come near to the door of her house" (Prov. 5:8) they refer to a whore.

4. A. And how far is one to keep away?

B. Said R. Hisda, "Four cubits."

5. A. And how do rabbis [who do not concur with Jacob] interpret the verse, "You shall not bring the hire of a harlot . . . into the house of the Lord your God" (Dt. 23:19)?

B. *They interpret it in accord with R. Hisda, for* said R. Hisda, "In the end every whore who hires herself out will hire out a man, as it is said, 'And in that you pay a hire and no hire is given to you, thus you are reversed' (Ez. 16:34)."

6. A. *[Referring to 4.B] that measurement differs from the opinion of R. Pedat, for* said R. Pedat, "The Torah has declared forbidden close approach only in the case of incest: 'None of you shall approach to any that is near of kin to him to uncover their nakedness' (Lev. 18:6)."

7. A. *When Ulla would come home from the household of the master, he would kiss his sisters on their hand.*

B. *Some say, "On their breast."*

C. *He then contradicts what he himself has said, for* said Ulla, "Even merely coming near is forbidden, as we say to the Nazirite, 'Go, go around about, but do not even come near the vineyard.' "

8. A. "The horse leech has two daughters: Give, give" (Prov. 30:15)—

B. *What is the meaning of* "Give, give"?

C. Said Mar Uqba, "It is the voice of the two daughters who cry out from Gehenna, saying to this world, 'Bring, bring.' *And who are they? They are minut and the government.*"

D. There are those who say, said R. Hisda said Mar Uqba, "It is the voice of Gehenna that is crying out, saying, 'Bring

me the two daughters who cry out from
Gehenna, saying to this world, 'Bring,
bring.' "

9. A. "None who to to her return, nor
do they attain the paths of life" (Prov.
2:19):

B. Now since they never return, how
are they going to attain the paths of life
anyhow?

C. *This is the sense of the passage,* "But if
they return, they will not attain the
paths of life."

D. *Does that then bear the implication that
whoever departs from minut dies? And lo,
there is the case of a certain woman who
came before R. Hisda and said to him, "The
lightest sin that she ever committed was that
her younger son is the child of her older
son."*

E. *And R. Hisda said to her, "So get busy
and prepare shrouds."*

F. *But she did not die. Now since she had
said that her lightest sin was that her
younger son is the child of her older son, it
must follow that she had also gone over to
minut [but she didn't die].*

G. *That one did not entirely revert, so that
is why she did not die [in this world,
leaving her to suffer in the world to come].*

H. *There are those who say, it is only from
minut that one dies if one repents, but not
from any other sin? And lo, there is the case
of a certain woman who came before R.*

Hisda, who said to her, "So get busy and prepare shrouds." And she died.

I. *Since she said that that was the lightest of her sins, it follows that she was guilty also of minut.*

10. A. *And if one renounces sins other than minut, does one not die? And has it not been taught on Tannaite authority:*

B. They say concerning R. Eleazar b. Dordia that he did not neglect a single whore in the world with whom he did not have sexual relations. One time he heard that there was a certain whore in one of the overseas towns, and she charged as her fee a whole bag of denars. He took a bag of denars and went and for her sake crossed seven rivers. At the time that he was with her, she farted, saying, "Just as this fart will never return to its place, so Eleazar b. Dordia will never be accepted in repentance."

C. He went and sat himself down between two high mountains and said, "Mountains and hills, seek mercy in my behalf."

D. They said to him, "Before we seek mercy for you, we have to seek mercy for ourselves: 'For the mountains shall depart and the hills be removed' (Is. 54:10)."

E. He said, "Heaven and earth, seek mercy for me."

F. They said to him, "Before we seek mercy for you, we have to seek mercy for ourselves: 'the heavens shall vanish away like smoke, and the earth shall wax old like a garment' (Is. 51:6)."

G. He said, "Sun and moon, seek mercy for me."

H. They said to him, "Before we seek mercy for you, we have to seek mercy for ourselves: 'Then the moon shall be confounded and the sun ashamed' (Is. 24:23)."

I. He said, "Stars and constellations, seek mercy for me."

J. They said to him, "Before we seek mercy for you, we have to seek mercy for ourselves: 'All the hosts of heaven shall molder away' (Is. 34:4)."

K. He said, "The matter depends only on me." He put his head between his knees and he wept a mighty weeping until his soul expired. An echo came forth and said, "R. Eleazar b. Dordia is destined for the life of the world to come."

L. *Now here was a case of a sin [other than minut] and yet he did die.*

M. *There too, since he was so much*

given over to that sin, it was as bad as minut.

N. [Upon hearing this story] Rabbi wept and said, "There is he who acquires his world in a single moment, and there is he who acquires his world in so many years."

O. And said Rabbi, "It is not sufficient for penitents to be received, they even that are called 'rabbi.' "

11. A. *R. Hanina and R. Jonathan were going along the way and came to a crossroads, with one road that led by the door of a temple of idol worship, the other by a whorehouse. Said one to the other, "Let's go by the road that passes the door of the temple of idol worhsip,* **[17B]** *for in any case the impulse that leads to that in our case has been annihilated."*

B. The other said to him, "Let's go by the road that passes the door of the whorehouse and overcome our impulse, and so gain a reward."

C. *[That is what they did.] When they came near the whorehouse, they saw the whores draw back at their presence. The other then said to him, "How did you know that this would happen?"*

D. He said to him, " 'She shall watch over you against lewdness, discernment shall guard you' (Prov. 2:11)."

12. A. [As to the verse, "She shall
watch over you against lewdness,
discernment shall guard you"
(Prov. 2:11),] said rabbis to Raba,
"What is the meaning of the word
translated 'lewdness'? Shall it be
'the Torah,' since the word
translated lewdness in the Aramaic
translation is rendered, 'it is a
counsel of the wicked' and
Scripture has the phrase,
'wonderful is his counsel and great
is his wisdom' (Is. 28:29)?
B. "Then the word should have
been written so as to yield
'lewdness.' Rather, this is the
sense of the verse: 'against things
of lewdness, discernment, the
Torah, shall watch over you.' "
13. A. *Our rabbis have taught on Tannaite
authority:*
B. When R. Eleazar b. Parta and R. Hanina
b. Teradion were arrested, R. Eleazar b.
Parta said to R. Hanina b. Teradion, "You
are fortunate, for you have been arrested on
only one count. Woe is me, that I have been
arrested on five counts."
C. Said to him R. Hanina, "You are
fortunate, for you have been arrested on five
counts but you will be saved, while woe is
me, for although I have been arrested on
only one count, I will not be rescued. For
you have devoted yourself to the study of

the Torah and also acts of beneficence, while I devoted myself only to the study of the Torah alone."

D. *And that accords with R. Huna, for* said R. Huna, "Whoever devotes himself only to the study of Torah alone is like one who has no God, as it is said, 'Now for long seasons Israel was without the true God' (2 Chr. 15:3). What is the meaning of 'without the true God'? It means that whoever devotes himself only to the study of Torah alone is like one who has no God."

E. But did he not engage in acts of beneficence as well? *And has it not been taught on Tannaite authority:*

F. R. Eliezer b. Jacob says, "A person should not hand over his money to the charity box unless it is under the supervision of a disciple of sages such as R. Hanina b. Teradion."

G. *While people did place their trust in him, he did not, in fact, carry out acts of beneficence.*

H. But has it not been taught on Tannaite authority, [R. Hanina b. Teradion, who was in charge of the community fund] said to [R. Yosé b. Qisma], "Money set aside for the celebration of Purim got confused for me with money set aside for charity, and I divided it all up for the poor [including my own funds]"?

I. *Well, while he did carry out acts of beneficence, he did not do so much as he was supposed to have done.*

J. *They brought R. Eleazar b. Parta and said to him, "How come you have repeated Mishnah traditions and how come you have been a thief?"*
K. *He said to them, "If a thief, then not a scribe, and if a scribe, then not a thief, and as I am not the one, so I am not the other."*
L. *"Then how come they call you 'rabbi'?"*
M. *"I am the rabbi of the weavers."*
N. *They brought him two coils of wool and asked, "Which is the warp and which is the woof?"*
O. *A miracle happened, and a she-bee came and sat on the warp and a he-bee came and sat on the woof, so he said, "This is the warp and that is the woof."*
P. *They said to him, "And how come you didn't come to the temple [literally: 'house of destruction']?"*
Q. *He said to them, "I am an elder, and I was afraid that people would trample me under their feet."*
R. *"And up to now how many old people have been trampled?"*
S. *A miracle happened, and on that very day an old man was trampled.*
T. *"And how come you freed your slave?"*
U. *He said to them, "No such thing took place."*
V. *One of them was about to get up to give testimony against him, when Elijah came and appeared to him in the form of one of the important lords of the government and said to that man, "Just as miracles were done for him in*

*all other matters, a miracle is going to happen in
this one, and you will turn out to be a common
scold."*

W. *But he paid no attention to him and got up
to address them, and a letter from important
members of the government had to be sent to the
Caesar, and it was through that man that it was
sent; on the road Elijah came and threw him four
hundred parasangs, so he went and never came
back.*

X. *They brought R. Hanina b. Teradion and said
to them, "How come you devoted yourself to the
Torah?"*

Y. He said to them, "It was as the Lord my
God has commanded me."

Z. Forthwith they made the decree that he
was to be put to death by burning, his wife
to be killed, and his daughter to be assigned
to a whorehouse.

AA. He was sentenced to be burned to
death, for he **[18A]** had pronounced the
divine name as it is spelled out.

BB. *But how could he have done such a thing,
and have we not learned in the Mishnah:* **All
Israelites have a share in the world to come,
as it is said, Your people also shall be all
righteous, they shall inherit the land
forever; the branch of my planting, the
work of my hands, that I may be glorified
(Is. 60:21). And these are the ones who have
no portion in the world to come: (1) He who
says, the resurrection of the dead is a
teaching which does not derive from the**

Torah, (2) and the Torah does not come from Heaven; and (3) an Epicurean. R. Aqiba says, "Also: He who reads in heretical books, and he who whispers over a wound and says, I will put none of the diseases upon you which I have put on the Egyptians, for I am the Lord who heals you (Ex. 15 :26)."Abba Saul says, "Also: he who pronounces the divine name as it is spelled out" [M. San. 10:1A-G]!

CC. He did it for practice. *For so it has been taught on Tannaite authority:*

DD. "You shall not learn to do after the abominations of those nations" (Dt. 18:9)—but you may learn about them so as to understand and to teach what they are.

EE. *Then why was he subjected to punishment?*

FF. It was because he repeated the divine name in public.

GG. And why was his wife sentenced to be put to death?

HH. *Because she did not stop him.*

II. On that account they have said: Whoever has the power to prevent someone from sinning and does not do so is punished on account of the other.

JJ. And why was his daughter sentenced to a whorehouse?

KK. For said R. Yohanan, "One time his daughter was walking before the great authorities of Rome. They said, 'How beautiful are the steps of this maiden,' and she forthwith became meticulous about her walk.

LL. *And that is in line with what R. Simeon b. Laqish said, "What is the meaning of that which is written,* 'The iniquity of my heel compasses me about' (Ps. 49:6)? The sins that a person treads under heel in this world surround him on the day of judgment."

MM. When three of them went out, they accepted the divine decree. He said, "The rock, his work is perfect, for all his ways are justice" (Dt. 32:4).

OO. His wife said, "A God of faithfulness and without iniquity, just and right is he" (Dt. 32:4).

PP. His daughter said, "Great in counsel and mighty in deed, whose eyes are open on all the ways of the sons of men, to give everyone according to his ways and according to the fruit of his deeds" (Jer. 32:19).

QQ. Said Rabbi, "How great are these righteous. For it was for their sake that these verses, which justify God's judgment, were made ready for the moment of the acceptance of God's judgment."

14. A. *Our rabbis have taught on Tannaite authority:*

B. When R. Yosé b. Qisma fell ill, R. Hanina b. Teradion went to visit him. He said to him, "Hanina, my brother, don't you know that from Heaven have they endowed this nation [Rome] with dominion? For [Rome] has destroyed his house, burned his Temple, slain his pious ones, and annihilated his very best—and yet endures! And yet I have heard about you that you go into session and devote yourself to the Torah and even call assemblies in public, with a scroll lying before you in your bosom."

C. He said to him, "May mercy be shown from heaven."

D. He said to him, "I am telling you sensible things, and you say to me, 'May mercy be shown from heaven'! I should be surprised if they do not burn up in fire both you and the scroll of the Torah."

E. He said to him, "My lord, what is my destiny as to the life of the age to come?"

F. He said to him, "Has some particular act come to hand [that leads you to concern]?"

G. He said to him, "Money set aside for the celebration of Purim got confused for me with money set aside for charity, and I divided it all up for the poor [including my own funds]."

H. He said to him, "If so, out of the portion that is coming to you may be the portion that is coming to me, and may my portion come from your portion."

I. They say: the days were no more than a few before R. Yosé b. Qisma died and all of the leading Romans went to bury him and they provided for him a splendid eulogy. And when they returned, they found R. Hanina b. Teradion in session and devoted

to the Torah, having called assemblies in
public, with a scroll lying before him in his
bosom. So they brought him and wrapped
him in a scroll of the Torah and surrounded
him with bundles of branches and set them
on fire. But they brought tufts of wool,
soaked in water, and put them on his chest,
so that he would not die quickly.

J. Said to him his daughter, "Father, how
can I see you this way?"

K. He said to her, "If I were being burned
all by myself, it would be a hard thing for
me to bear. But now that I am being burned
with a scroll of the Torah with me, he who
will exact punishment for the humiliation
brought on the scroll of the Torah is the one
who will seek vengeance for the humiliation
brought on me."

L. Said to him his disciples, "My lord, what
do you see?"

M. He said to them, "The parchment is
burned, but the letters fly upward."

N. "You too—open your mouth and let the
fire in [so that you will die quickly]."

O. He said to them, "It is better that the
one who gave [life] take it away, but let a
person not do injury to himself."

P. The executioner said to him, "My lord, if
I make the flames stronger and remove the
tufts of wool from your chest, will you bring
me into the life of the world to come?"

Q. He said to him, "Yes."

R. He said to him, "Will you take an oath to me?"

S. He took an oath to him. Forthwith he made the flames stronger and removed the tufts of wool from his chest, so his soul rapidly departed. Then the other leapt into the flames. An echo came forth and said, "R. Hanina b. Teradion and the executioner are selected for the life of the world to come."

T. Rabbi wept and said, "There is he who acquires his world in a single moment, and there is he who acquires his world in so many years."

15. A. *Beruriah, the wife of R. Meir, was the daughter of R. Hanina b. Teradion. She said to him, "It is humiliating for me that my sister should be put into a whorehouse."*

B. *He took a tarqab full of denars and went. He said, "If a prohibited act has not been done to her, then a miracle will happen, and if she has done something prohibited, no miracle will happen to her."*

C. *He went and took on the guise of a horseman. He said, "Submit to me."*

D. *She said to him, "I am menstruating."*

E. *He said to her, "I'll wait."*

F. *She said to him, "There are plenty of girls here who are prettier than I am."*

G. *He said, "That means the woman has not done anything prohibited, that's what she says to everybody."*

H. *He went to her guard and said to him, "Give her to me."*

I. *He said to him, "I'm afraid of the government."*

J. *He said to him, "Take this tarqab of denars, half as a bribe, the other half for you."*

K. *He said to him, "What shall I do when these are used up?"*

L. *"Just say, 'Let the God of Meir answer me,' and you'll be saved."*

M. *He said to him,* **[18B]** *"And who will tell me that that's so?"*

N. *He said to him, "You'll now see." There were these dogs, who would bite people. He took a stone and threw it at them, and when they were going to bite him, he said, "God of Meir, answer me," and they left him alone.*

O. *So he handed her over to him. But eventually the matter became known at government house, and when the guard was brought and taken to the gallows, he exclaimed, "God of Meir, answer me."*

P. *They took him down from the gallows and asked him, "What's going on?"*

Q. *He told him, "This is what happened."*

R. *They then incised the likeness of R. Meir at the gate of Rome, saying, "Whoever sees this face, bring him here."*

S. *One day they saw him and pursued him. He ran from them and went into a whorehouse. Some say he just happened then to see food cooked by gentiles and dipped in one finger and then sucked another [pretending he was a gentile]. Others say*

that Elijah the prophet appeared to them as a
harlot and embraced him (God forbid). So they
said, "If this were R. Meir, he would never have
done such a thing."
T. *He went and fled to Babylonia. Some say, it*
was because of that incident that he fled to
Babylonia, others, it was because of the incident
with Beruria [who committed adultery with one
of his disciples].

Nos. 3, 4, 5, and 6 form footnotes to no. 2 or to
one another. No. 7 is a footnote to no. 6. No. 8 then
reverts to the general theme of the interplay of the
government and *minut*. No. 9 then continues the
theme of no. 8, which is the return of those who
have gone over to *minut* and ended up in Gehenna.
No. 10 goes forward along the same theme, though
with a fresh composition. The issue once more is
whether or not one may atone and so die and enter
the world to come for the sin of *minut*, or whether
one has to live out his years and then go to Gehenna. This forms part of a large-scale set of compositions on the common theme at hand. No. 11
proceeds along the line of the established theme:
the sin of idolatry compared with other sins. No.
12 is a footnote to no. 11. The general theme of rabbis' arrests by the Romans explains why the next
composition has been included; this brings us back
to the interest of no. 2 and marks the end of the
secondary expansion of the story about Eliezer. So
each large-scale composite that forms a subdivision
of the whole commences with a Tannaite formation, followed by a collection of secondary expan-

sions of various kinds. The inclusion of no. 13 then makes sense within the framework of discourse established by no. 2. Nos. 14 and 15 provide yet other stories involving Hanina b. Teradion and belong to the same prepared sequence of stories about him.

Here is then a splendid example of the forming of a composite for one clearly indicated purpose, and its utilization—quite tangentially—for another. II.2 forms the beginning of a large and beautifully crafted set of materials on a general theme, bearing a specific proposition. The general theme is the relationship of sages to the Roman government. The specific proposition is that there are two sources of danger to one's immortal soul: dealing with *minut* (not defined, but in this context, certainly some Christianity or another), and dealing with the government. The first part of the composite deals with former; the second, the latter. There is no mixing the one with the other, but, of course, dealing with *minut* involves government sanctions, as much as rebellion against the government itself. No. 2, carrying in its wake nos. 3, 4, and 5, as glosses and extensions, and bearing as footnotes nos. 6 and 7, form one cogent subdivision. No. 8 then provides a transition to the next, which will draw our attention to the dangers involved in dealing with the government. Is there a unifying theme throughout? Of course there is, and it involves the proposition that dealing with *minut* endangers one's soul, while, if one violates the policy of the government, one may lose his or her life, but thereby, in any event, will gain the life of the world to come. No. 10 shows us a fully articulated composition, obviously completed in its own terms and for its author's own purpose, which has been inserted, with good reason. Nos. 13, 14, and 15, another obviously well-crafted set of stories, each made up in its own terms, but all of them working together in common cause, then form the conclusion, balancing the opening units.

Now do I maintain that all of these materials have been made up merely to amplify a reference to the judge's tribunal? Obviously not. What challenge to the ingenuity of a compositor would such a purpose have presented? Mere amplification on a theme is too easy, too trivial a task. To the contrary, we have here a variety of compositions, some of them bearing their own burden of secondary expansion, clarification, and complement, others not. If we were to ask, Have these compositions been made up for the purposes of a composite of such materials?, the obvious answer is, probably yes, but not for this composite in particular! The probability is that authors wrote up stories for collections meant to make a given point, serve a given purpose. To say that these formed "biographical collections," or "biographies" seems to me to make a rather banal statement.

But it is a wrong one too, since there is hardly an interest in a sustained life of a sage. To the contrary, the types of story here serve not biography but a different purpose altogether, which is, a handbook of lessons to be learned if one is to live the life of a sage within the model of the sage: how to deal with the government, how to avoid the

111

temptations of *minut,* and the like. But if people were working on such compilations of exemplary stories, serving to make points important in the education of the sage—a handbook for the disciple of the sage in particular, in the way in which tractate Avot is a handbook for the disciple of the sage— then the work led nowhere. For we have massive compilations of such compositions, but—as shown in the Bavli before us—no freestanding composites that gain entry into the Bavli to serve the particular purpose for which such composites were originally made up. A process of composition and compilation of compositions into composites yielded what is before us. But the whole has found its location here not only because of the adventitious point of intersection with what is of interest to the Bavli's framers, which is the exposition (here) of a detail of the Mishnah: what is the judge's tribunal.

The composite transcends the precipitating cause for the formation of the composite: it makes a much larger point, and in connecting this to that to the other thing to make that point, the framers have signaled a still larger and more important judgment on the nature of things. What begins as a fairly technical statement on the furniture of the courtroom rapidly expands into a complex and subtle formation of discrete but intersecting themes. We start with a catalog of things we do not sell the gentiles, meaning, in this case, their governments. Israel is not to help the nations build the instruments of power, including those for the governance of the social order—scaffold, stadium, judges' tribunal, for instance. Now if we ask ourselves what general theme is introduced in these details, it is Israel's corporate relationship to the corporate being of gentile society. Then what of the story of Eliezer? It is not so much an explanation of the detail about the judge's tribunal, as it is an extreme claim that even good things that gentiles (here, Christians) know, even legitimate learnings from the Torah that they may have in hand, are to be shunned. The near-at-hand enemy, the brother, presents the greatest threat, and a long sequence of stories about *minut* then follows. The next major initiative, commencing at no. 13, explains how Israelites are to conduct themselves when facing the sanctions of the gentile state (clearly: not a Christian government here, since that is no longer a major motif). The powerful formulation of the choices in public policy facing Israel—(1) don't you know that from Heaven have they endowed this nation [Rome] with dominion? For [Rome] has destroyed his house, burned his Temple, slain his pious ones, and annihilated his very best—and yet endures!, or (2) May mercy be shown from heaven, meaning, God will resolve such matters—sets forth the alternatives. So a long and complex formation in fact holds together to treat a single problem and to make only a few points about that subject. The palimpsest in the end is subject to a single reading; the bore, top to bottom, brings up not mere detritus, the random sediment of passage ages, but a single solid rock. In a stunning composite such as this, the social policy of Israel comes to full formation.

So much for the cogency of a complex discourse—cogency in the statement of a proposition, not merely in the episodic establishment of connections between one thing and something else. Before us here and in the other examples in these pages is a thematic composite that sets forth a proposition—not merely a sequence of lexical entries (so to speak) or encyclopedia articles, but an essay in the great tradition of well-expounded thought. True, the Bavli's authors and compositors with the best will in the world cannot gain entry into the august salon of the great philosophical writers of the ages, and I cannot claim that Plato need fear the competition—let alone envy the craft—of our (so deeply admired) sages of blessed memory. But by another criterion than the one of aesthetic elegance as we in the Christian and Greek traditions of the West define elegance, another accomplishment, by which form in words recapitulates a social perception, may win appreciation. I refer to the way in which, in their public, anonymous writing, meant as the foundation-document for the social order, the composition of thought corresponds to the character of society. What I offer is a mere guess, an observation that may prove plausible but that—like particle physics—lies beyond the possibility (at this time at least) of demonstration through probative experiment.

If we stand back and consider the condition of Israel as the framers of the Bavli understood it, what do we see? Our sages of blessed memory, who produced the Talmud of Babylonia, knew that "Israel" required quotation marks, as a construct and fabrication, with slight evidence in the workaday world to justify the formation of such a social entity within a theory of world order. For "Israel" was not one thing but many things. First, "Israel" was not in some one place. The framers of the Talmud explicitly recognized that (not Jews but) "Israel" lived in a great many places, alongside gentiles. At most, some villages were made up mostly, or entirely, of "Israel." They lived on both sides of the always contested frontier between Iran and Rome, and at many places within the Roman Empire as well. By the advent of the seventh century, it is clear, "Israel" was present also in Armenia, to the north and west of Babylonia, in eastern provinces of Iran, outward toward India further to the east, and in what we know now as Afghanistan, Tadzhikistan, and other territories to the northeast, en route to China. The silk trade, in which we know Jews took part, carried Israel ever nearer to China. As to the west, the Bavli's writers were well aware that Jews lived not only in Asia Minor, but also in Italy proper and in Spain to the far west. So what is this "Israel"anyhow, being nearly ubiquitous but never coherent?

The geography of "Israel" in distant places corresponded to the political and social stratigraphy of "Israel" close at hand. Without following our sages' example and providing rather more information than the argument requires, I state simply that the authors of the Talmud knew two sources of politics nearby: the Iranians' recognized ruler of Jewry, whom the Jews knew as the *exilarch*, on the one side, and the sages' own (subordinated) courts and administration of small matters in the villages, on the other. These two sources of legitimate coercion within "Israel" in the sages' view competed and in no way complemented one another (though I suspect the exilarch will have seen matters in a different, and more irenic, way). "Israel" spoke more than a single language (Aramaic), and on a few occasions, Iranian-speaking Jews crop up in the pages of the Bavli, as do Greek-speaking ones in the counterpart Talmud of the Land of Israel. And that "Israel" encompassed rich and poor, farmer and merchant, slave and master, man and woman, hardly requires demonstration. If, therefore, I had to invent an aesthetic for discursive writing that would correspond in the formation of sentences, paragraphs, and chapters to the social order the writing was meant to portray, it would be difficult to imagine a more appropriate medium for setting forth ideas than the composite: composite writing for a diverse and disorderly social world beyond. Like a symphony in time of war — Shostakovich's seventh on Leningrad under siege, for example — which evokes in sound the roar of battle, or like a poem which in form captures the poet's unease beneath a surface of simple repose — Frost's "Stopping by Woods on a Snowy Evening" is a case in point — so a sustained and massive statement can speak at more levels than the level of what is articulated. And, underneath, the disjunctive and disrupted formations — this, then that, but also the other thing — can indeed replicate a mode of thought singularly appropriate to a distinctive society and its composite character: discrete, diverse, composite indeed, yet, seen from the proper perspective, coherent and bearing a single message. The right perspective, of course, must be from an adequate distance—on high, for instance.

What makes me propose that the particular program for the formation of composites bears evidence of a broader conception of the social order in the minds of the framers of composites? It is the compelling force of a ubiquitous premise: people beyond the writers will not only understand the writing but—perhaps in an inchoate and unarticulated way—find self-evidence in the character of the writing. Hence the conception of what naturally formed connections to something else signals the assumption that what to the writer seemed cogent to the reader or listener would be cogent. Rules of composition that define the correct rhetoric for the expression of a thought in proper syntax and grammar and formal structure and the useful logic govern how people write cogent thought, not only how they draw together diverse available writings within a larger statement. The guess that the way in which people write conveys the image of how they experience the social world brings to actuality my conviction, a mere perspective, a scarcely examined attitude that just as personal writing mirrors the private world, so public writing mirrors the social world.

No one doubts that the great inventors of poetry and fiction begin within, forming of words an account of a world that commences in the privacy of the heart, the personality of the unique intellect. To maintain that an anonymous writing, intended to state in words the structure and order of the social world, has been crafted in the same way—first

from world to words, then from words to world—
is to argue merely by appealing to analogy. And
yet, it is the simple fact that to represent "Israel" in
words, one could find no more accurate a medium
for replication in sentence structure of the social order than the composite, for that is what Israel was,
and would remain, through time. But if the medium responded to the social order, the message
would stand only for our sages of blessed memory.

Part Three

The Law Behind
the Laws

Chapter 4

Saying the Same Thing About Many Things: The Bavli and the Perfection of the Mishnah

In many ways and about many things our sages of blessed memory found it possible to say one thing, and that was the law behind the laws that formed their stock in trade. Accordingly, I use the word "law" in the way in which in systematic learning (*Wissenschaft, scienza, science,* in German, Italian, and French) the word is meant, that is, "laws of science" formulate and describe the generalization which emerges from many cases: what is regular, orderly, and useful in the further discovery of knowledge in the examination of many more cases.[1] Now, if the Bavli's form—as I maintain—responded to the social world beyond, so that the foundation-document under construction comprised a formation, within mind, of a world out there, what law was that form meant to formulate? If the writing represented an experiment in the aesthetics of the intellectual deconstruction and reconstruction of the everyday, the medium carried a message meant to frame and reform the everyday.

The Bavli made a single statement through many

---

1. By law in this context I mean not the jurisprudential principle that is expressed through a variety of cases, but rather the law of science, the law of life.

statements, and that is the "law" of the Bavli. A piece of writing crying out for a good editor, or a bit of self-discipline, the Bavli's cruel repetition, its tedium, and its redundancy required thoughtful readers to find a single law within many laws. That law, we shall see, in no way derived from society, or, on the surface, even pertained to it. Ours is a rather odd foundation-document for society, since as we shall see in due course, the "law" of the Bavli did not concern society at all. It concerned the Mishnah, and the law beyond the laws of the Mishnah. For the foundation-document of the Bavli, the Mishnah, demonstrably was intended to say one thing about many things. And since, as a matter of fact, the principal and generative law which the framers of the Bavli presented through numerous cases concerned the Mishnah, understanding the law of the Bavli requires that we understand both the method and the message of the Mishnah. Unpacking these simple allegations takes two steps. I have first of all to show how a document through saying many things really says one thing in many ways. That document of course must be the Mishnah. Then, second, I have to identify what it is that the Bavli, for its part, never articulates but always states in connection with the Mishnah. The former work occupies the remainder of this chapter; the latter, the next.

That is why, in order to demonstrate how a large and encompassing document may speak of many things but say only one thing, I turn to the Mishnah. And that is necessary, because the Bavli, in form, presents itself as a commentary to the Mishnah, and one principal message of the Bavli, the one given priority throughout, concerns the Mishnah. So if, as I allege, the Bavli forms the foundation-document of the society of Israel, it speaks not of the social order of Israel but only the literary reality of the Mishnah—a very strange way of setting forth a design for the composite nation and its complex society.

The Mishnah is a document that says the same thing over and over again—not only iterating but also demonstrating a single proposition. The telos of thought in the Mishnah is such that many things are made to say one thing which concerns the nature of being. The Mishnah iterates throughout that all things are not only orderly, but ordered in such wise that many things fall into one classification, and one thing may hold together many things of diverse classifications. These two matched and complementary propositions—many things are one, one thing encompasses many—compelement each other, because, in forming matched opposites, the two provide a single, complete, and final judgment of the whole of being, social, natural, supernatural alike. The Mishnah's rationality consists in that sense of hierarchy that orders all things in one and the same way. That rationality appeals, moreover, to the nature of things for its demonstration. For it is revealed time and again, as we have seen at tedious length, by the possibility always of effecting the hierarchical classification of all things: each thing in its taxon, all taxa in correct sequence, from least to greatest.

Showing that all things can be ordered, and that all orders can be set into relationship with one another, we of course transform method into message. The Mishnah's message concerns the encompassing hierarchical classification of all being. It is that many things really form a single thing, the many species a single genus, the many genera an encompassing and well-crafted, cogent whole. And that whole is made up of the orderly hierarchization of the parts, this to the next, the next to the one beyond, upward to God at the apex. Every time we speciate but then hierarchize the species, we affirm that position. Each successful labor of forming relationships among species—e.g., making them into a genus, or identifying the hierarchy of the species—proves it again. Not only so, but when we can show that many things are really one, or that one thing yields many (the reverse and confirmation of the former), we say in a fresh way a single immutable truth, the one of this philosophy concerning the unity of all being in an orderly composition of all things within a single taxon. Exegesis always is repetitive—and a sound exegesis of the systemic exegesis must then be equally so, everywhere explaining the same thing in the same way.

To show how this exegesis of mine works, I turn to only one component of the matter, devoted to the sustained effort to demonstrate how many classes of things—actions, relationships, circumstances, persons, places—are demonstrated really to form one class. Just as God, in creation, ordered all things, each in its class under its name, so in the Mishnah classification works its way through the potentialities of chaos to explicit order. As in the miracle of God's creation of the world in six days, here too is classification transformed from the *how* of intellection to the *why* and the *what for* and, above all, the *what-does-it-all-mean*. Now speaking of God in the context of the Mishnah proves jarring, for God is not at issue. The issue concerns nature, not supernature, and sorts out and sifts the everyday data of the here and the now. It will prove its points, therefore, by appeal to the palpable facts of creation, which everyone knows and can test. So recognition that one thing may fall into several categories and many things into a single one comes to expression, for the authorship of the Mishnah, in secular ways.[2]

If we can show that differentiation flows from *within* what is differentiated — that is, from the intrinsic or inherent traits of things — then we confirm that at the heart of things is a fundamental ontological being, single, cogent, simple, that is capable of diversification, yielding complexity and diversity. The upshot is to be stated with emphasis: *That diversity in species or diversification in actions follows orderly lines confirms the claim that there is that single point from which many lines come forth.* Carried out in proper order — (1) the many form one thing, and (2) one thing yields many — the demonstration then leaves no doubt as to the truth of the matter. Ideally, therefore, we shall argue from the simple to the complex, showing that the one yields the many; one thing, many things; two, four.

---

2. I of course use the word *secular* in a very precise sense.

MISHNAH-TRACTATE SHABBAT 1:1

1:1 A. [Acts of] transporting objects from one domain to another, [which violate] the Sabbath, (1) are two, which [indeed] are four [for one who is] inside, (2) and two which are four [for one who is] outside,

B. How so?

C. [If on the Sabbath] the beggar stands outside and the householder inside,

D. [and] the beggar stuck his hand inside and put [a beggar's bowl] into the hand of the householder,

E. or if he took [something] from inside it and brought it out,

F. the beggar is liable, the householder is exempt.

G. [If] the householder stuck his hand outside and put [something] into the hand of the beggar,

H. or if he took [something] from it and brought it inside,

I. the householder is liable, and the beggar is exempt.

J. [If] the beggar stuck his hand inside, and the householder took [something] from it,

K. or if [the householder] put something in it and he [the beggar] removed

L. both of them are exempt.

M. [If] the householder put his hand outside and the beggar took [something] from it,

N. or if [the beggar] put something into it and [the householder] brought it back inside,

O. both of them are exempt.

M. Shab. 1:1 classifies diverse circumstances of transporting objects from private to public domain. The purpose is to assess the rules that classify as culpable or exempt from culpability diverse arrangements. The operative point is that a prohibited action is culpable only if one and the same person commits the whole of the violation of the law. If two or more people share in the single action, neither of them is subject to punishment. At stake therefore is the conception that one thing may be many things, and if that is the case, then culpability is not incurred by any one actor.

The consequence of showing that one thing is many things is set forth with great clarity in the consideration not of the actor but of the action. One class of actions is formed by those that violate the sanctity of the Sabbath. Do these form many subdivisions, and, if so, what difference does it make? Here is a passage that shows how a single class of actions yields multiple and complex speciation, while remaining one:[3]

MISHNAH-TRACTATE SHABBAT 7:1–2

7:1 A. A general rule did they state concerning the Sabbath:

B. Whoever forgets the basic principle of the Sabbath and performed many acts of labor on many different Sabbath days is liable only for a single sin offering.

---

3. This is one of my favorites, among many. In my view, the whole of the Mishnah's method, seen with great precision as philosophical in program and logic, legal in idiom and expression, is typified by this wonderful and deservedly famous pericope.

C. He who knows the principle of the Sabbath and performed many acts of labor on many different Sabbaths is liable for the violation of each and every Sabbath.

D. He who knows that it is the Sabbath and performed many acts of labor on many different Sabbaths is liable for the violation of each and every generative category of labor.

E. He who performs many acts of labor of a single type is liable only for a single sin offering.

7:2 A. The generative categories of acts of labor [prohibited on the Sabbath] are forty less one:

B. (1) he who sews, (2) ploughs, (3) reaps, (4) binds sheaves, (5) threshes, (6) winnows, (7) selects [fit from unfit produce or crops], (8) grinds, (9) sifts, (10) kneads, (11) bakes;

C. (12) he who shears wool, (13) washes it, (14) beats it, (15) dyes it;

D. (16) spins, (17) weaves,

E. (18) makes two loops, (19) weaves two threads, (20) separates two threads;

F. (21) ties, (22) unties,

G. (23) sews two stitches, (24) tears in order to sew two stitches;

H. (25) he who traps a deer, (26) slaughters it, (27) flays it, (28) salts it, (29) cures its hide, (30) scrapes it, and (31) cuts it up;

I. (32) he who writes two letters, (33) erases two letters in order to write two letters;

J. (34) he who builds, (35) tears down;

K. (36) he who puts out a fire, (37) kindles a
fire;

L. (38) he who hits with a hammer; (39) he
who transports an object from one domain to
another—

M. lo, these are the forty generative acts of
labor less one.

Now we see how the fact that one thing yields
many things confirms the philosophy of the unity
of all being. For the many things all really are one
thing, here, the intrusion into sacred time of actions that do not belong there. M. Shab. 7:1–2
presents a parallel to the discussion, in Mishnah-
tractate Sanhedrin, of how many things can be
shown to be one thing and to fall under a single rule,
and how one thing may be shown to be many things
and to invoke multiple consequences. It is that interest at M. 7:1 which accounts for the inclusion of
M. 7:2, and the exposition of M. 7:2 occupies much
of the tractate that follows. Accordingly, just as at
Mishnah-tractate Sanhedrin the specification of the
many and diverse sins or felonies that are penal-
ized in a given way shows us how many things are
one thing and then draws in its wake the specification of those many things, so here we find a similar
exercise. It is one of classification, working in two
ways, then: the power of a unifying taxon, the
force of a differentiating and divisive one. The list
of the acts of labor then gives us the categories of
work, and performing any one of these constitutes
a single action in violation of the Sabbath.

How, exactly, do these things work themselves out? If one does not know that the Sabbath is incumbent upon him, then whatever he does falls into a single taxon. If he knows that the Sabbath exists and violates several Sabbath days in succession, what he does falls into another taxon. If one knows that the Sabbath exists in principle and violates it in diverse ways, e.g., through different types of prohibited acts of labor, then many things become still more differentiated. The consideration throughout, then, is how to assess whether something is a single or multiple action as to the reckoning of the consequence. So the species point to the genus, all classes to one class, all taxa properly hierarchized then rise to the top of the structure and the system forming one taxon. So all things ascend to, reach one thing. The law behind the laws of the Mishnah states: all things—in nature and society alike—are to be ordered in hierarchical classification. So much for a simple reprise of how the Mishnah says the same thing in many different ways.[4] Now to the message that the Talmud conveys not in so many words but in a great many examples.

The authors of the Bavli composed their writing in the form of a commentary to the Mishnah. So the very character of the Bavli tells us the sages' view of the Mishnah. The Bavli is portrayed as a commentary to the Mishnah, and at the commencement of most sustained discourses the fram-

---

4. For further discussion on this matter, see my *Judaism as Philosophy*.

ers placed comments on a given Mishnah sentence or paragraph. So the Mishnah presented itself to them as constitutive, the text of ultimate concern. That fact, so easily taken for granted, should surprise us. For other Judaisms did not present their laws as commentaries upon a prior code, e.g., Scripture. Building within the supplied framework of a received text is a mode of writing that other Judaisms of the same age and place did not practice. Secondary compositions upon an authoritative code outside of Scripture constituted a classification of writing difficult to identify outside of the realm of the Judaism of the dual Torah.[5]

---

5. Legal texts of the Essene library at Qumran, for instance, are framed as autonomous statements of ordinary rules and procedures, perhaps comparable with the Mishnah; these do not elicit secondary expansion and development, the accretion of sustained discourse, such as the Bavli reveals. Rules for an occasion such as those in the Manual of Discipline did not generate elaborate books of explanation and amplification. Books of ad hoc rules, so far as we know, were not venerated. So other Israelites, writing for other Judaisms, could and did write down rules without making the rule book into a focus of intellectual obsession, creating a line-by-line exegesis for a text, the way the Bavli's sages exalted the phrases and words of the Mishnah and so vastly expanded the whole into something larger and deeper than what it originally had been. Among whatever candidates, whether the Mishnah, the Manual of Discipline, the Elephantine papyri, or even the Holiness Code, the Priestly Code, and the Covenant Code of the Pentateuch, the mosaics of the written Torah, so far as we know, only the Mishnah received a Bavli. That fact is not difficult to interpret. The character of the Bavli presents us with the definitive context. The Bavli is a commentary written by philosopher-lawyers, men of extraordinary power to explain and amplify legal words and phrases, to generalize about rules, to theorize about matters of law as about mathematics. But in the mass of detail, a single point repeatedly was proved.

The principal and paramount proposition the framers of the Bavli set forth in infinite detail is that the Mishnah is a perfect piece of writing,[6] exhibiting no flaws such as mar the writings of ordinary men.[7] That proposition yielded two corollaries. First came the blatant and unsurprising principle that the Mishnah's construction of reality accurately portrayed how things really were, that is, the hierarchical classification of all being. What the Mishnah said in general, not only in detail here and there, was so. Second emerged the more subtle, because merely implicit, proposition. It was that the masters whose opinions are represented in the Mishnah—and, therefore, their disciples even

6. Scholars of early Islam may find interesting a comparison of the Bavli's claim of the perfection of the Mishnah and the Muslim characterization of the Quran as perfect.
7. The practical, ideological reason the sages deemed it urgent to do so, and with such extraordinary vigor and energy, must surely be that the Mishnah was the authoritative code for their courts. The exposition of the laws of the Mishnah demanded their best energies because the Mishnah's laws governed. Studied, therefore, in their circles of disciples, these laws defined both what was to be done and why sages, in particular, were the ones to do it. We do not know whether, from the very moment of its closure in 200, the Mishnah was entrusted to sages such as those represented in our Bavli, clerks in the administration of the Jewish nation in the Iranian millet system. Stories that say so do not settle the question. We know only this: four hundred years after the closure of the Mishnah, the Bavli came forth with its ample testimony to the concerns of philosopher-lawyers, who, in part, devoted their lives to clerkships in the Jewish government (such as it was) of their country. We have no adequate evidence to show just when these sages received the code and so found it necessary, for pressing, everyday reasons, to rework it into what they made of it. That they did receive and rework the Mishnah, we know only because we have the Bavli. So the work was done by people who needed to do the work in just the way they did it. From that simple supposition all else follows. Philosophers (if that is what they were) were drawn to this text, rather

down to the very present—were entirely consistent in what they said, so that the deepest premises
of their rulings cohered in a unitary composition
(not a composite), governing all things. The perfection of being in its hierarchical classification, to
which the Mishnah gave full exposure, found its
counterpart in the perfection of intellect characteristic of the document, on the one side, and its heirs
and interpreters, on the other.

So when the framers of the Bavli persistently
produced their proofs that every passage of the
Mishnah could be shown to cohere with all others
at each point of intersection, and, more, that the
premises that lay in the deepest structure of the
law comprised some few, simple facts governing
all being, they said a single thing through what
they said about many things. And what they said
pertained as much to themselves as to the Mishnah. What we see, therefore, is the intellectual val-
idation of a social fact: the position of sages at the
hierarchy of being, built, as it was, upon the apex
of Sinai. Here, once more, we see that the way in

than some other, because they were also lawyers. These lawyers'
profession centered upon an institution lacking analogy in our own
world and hence also lacking a suitable name in our language. We
call it simply an "institution." The institution was formed by masters with their disciples and subordinated specialists, such as pro-
fessional memorizers of traditions. The institution in part
intersected with the Jewish government of the country and so constituted a court or bureau of some sort. Certain activities of public
administration are well represented. So the institution intersected,
also, with the political system of the Jewish villages of Babylonia
and constituted a kind of inchoate municipality. But the institution
did not encompass the Jewish government, which comprised other
elements.

which writing was carried out corresponded in its form to the social imperatives of those doing the writing: the medium in its minute detail of style and recurrent form conveyed the message of the whole. And, by implication, the patterns of speech verified what was said.

In demonstrating the perfection of the Mishnah, our sages first of all exposed the scriptural sources or foundations for the rules of the Mishnah. For they everywhere implied that the Mishnah states in its way a principle that Scripture set down long ago. So the apologia commences with the insistent demonstration that the Mishnah derives from the principles revealed at Sinai, and hence comes from God. That demonstration then proves two facts. First, the Mishnah is subordinate to Scripture and its authorities' statements derived from verses of Scripture. But, second, the Mishnah, like Scripture, appeals in the end to God's giving of the Torah to Moses, our rabbi, at Sinai. Then what the Mishnah says may, formally, be shown to be based upon the written Torah. But what the Mishnah says may, in principle, be shown to state in a concrete circumstance a principle that also comes to expression in a concrete circumstance in the written Torah: both from Sinai, equally. In general, the former of the two propositions, the formal one, predominates.

A fixed rhetorical particle, *what is the source of this statement?*, is ordinarily used. The answer to that question invariably is, "as it is written," or equivalent citation language. The initial argument on the Mishnah's standing and authority therefore founded both upon the basis of the written Torah. The proof out of Scripture for a proposition of the Mishnah is illustrated in the following.[8] In line with what I said in part 2, I indent the secondary and tertiary additions, to show how the whole forms a single, cogent composite, complete with footnotes, and footnotes to footnotes.

1:8F–9

G. "They do not rent them houses in the Land of Israel,

H. "and, it goes without saying, fields. In Syria they rent houses to them, but not fields.

I. "And abroad they sell them houses and rent them fields," the words of R. Meir.

K. R. Yosé says, "In the land of Israel they rent them houses, but not fields;

L. "in Syria they sell them houses and rent them fields;

M. "and abroad they sell them both the one and the other."

M. 1:8

I.1 A. *What is the scriptural basis for this rule?*

B. Said R. Yosé bar Hanina, **[20A]** "It is because Scripture has said, '. . . nor be gracious to them,' [the letters of which can yield the phrase,] 'you shall not give them a place to settle on the ground.' "

C. *But that clause is required to make this point,*

---

8. There is a minor error of arrangement in the Talmud, since the Mishnah paragraph that is addressed is not the one (M. 1:8A–E) to which the passage is attached. To show how the matter is worked out, I give the correct Mishnah–paragraph.

which the All-Merciful wishes to set forth: "you
shall not admire their grace."

D. *If that were the case, then Scripture could as
well have used the passive tense. Why use the
active? That yields two points [the ones of B and
C].*

E. *Still, the phrase is required to make this point,
which the All-Merciful wishes to set forth:* "You
shall not give them gratuitous gifts."

F. *If that were the case, then Scripture could as
well have used different vowels [which would have
yielded that other meaning]. Why use the form we
have? That yields three points.*

2. A. *So too it has been taught on Tannaite
authority:*

B. ". . . nor be gracious to them:" [the letters
of which can yield the phrase,] "you shall not
give them a place to settle on the ground."

C. Another matter: ". . . nor be gracious to
them:" "you shall not admire their grace."

D. Another matter: ". . . nor be gracious to
them:" "You shall not give them gratuitous
gifts."

3. A. *But the matter of whether or not it is
permitted to give them gratuitous gifts is subject
to a conflict between Tannaite rulings. For it has
been taught on Tannaite authority:*

B. " 'You shall not eat of anything that dies
of itself; to the stranger that is within your
gates you may give it that he may eat it; or
you may sell it to a gentile' (Dt. 14:21)
["stranger" is one who has renounced

idolatry but does not yet observe the food taboos].

C. "I know only that one may give it to a stranger or sell it to a gentile. How on the basis of Scripture do I know that it may be sold to a gentile? Scripture says, 'You may give it . . . or sell it.' How do we know that you may give it to a gentile? Because Scripture says, 'You may give it that he may eat it or you may sell it to a gentile.' So it follows that both giving and selling pertain to both a stranger and a gentile," the words of R. Meir.

D. R. Judah says, "Matters are just as they are written out: to a foreigner the food is transferred as a gift, and to a gentile, through sale."

E. *But R. Meir's formulation makes perfectly good sense!*

F. *Now R. Judah may say to you, "If you think that matters are as R. Meir has stated them, then the All-Merciful ought to have written, 'you shall give it and he may eat, and sell it . . . .' Why does Scripture say, 'or sell it'? It is to indicate that matters are just as they are written out."*

G. *And R. Meir?*

H. *The formulation we have indicates that it is a priority to give it away to a stranger rather than sell it to a gentile.*

I. *And R. Judah?*

J. *Since in the case of a stranger, you are commanded to keep him alive, and concerning a Canaanite you are not commanded to keep him alive, it is hardly necessary to have a verse of Scripture to tell us to give priority to the stranger.*

4. A. ". . . nor be gracious to them:" "you shall not admire their grace."

B. *This supports the view of Rab, for* Rab has said, "It is forbidden to someone to say, 'How beautiful is that gentile!' "

C. *An objection was raised:* There is the case involving Rabban Simeon b. Gamaliel, who was on the steps of the Temple mount and saw an unusually beautiful gentile woman and said, "How great are your works, O Lord" (Ps. 104:24).

D. And so too, R. Aqiba saw the wife of the wicked Turnusrufus. He spit and laughed and wept. He spit, for she came from a rancid drop of semen; he laughed, because [he foresaw that] she was going to convert *and he would marry her;* and he wept, *because that beauty would end up in the dirt.*

E. *And Rab?*

F. *[In each case] the sage was giving thanks.* For a master has said, "He who sees good-looking people says, 'Blessed is he who has created such as these in his world.' "

5. A. *But is it permitted even to look? And an objection is to be raised:* "You shall keep from you every evil thing" (Dt. 23:10)— one should not stare at a beautiful woman, even if she is not married, or at a married woman, even if she is ugly, **[20B]** or at a woman's exquisite clothing; or at

male or female asses; or at a pig and a
sow; or at fowls when they are mating;
even if one is all eyes like the angel of
death.

    6. A. They say of the angel of death
that the whole of him is made up of
eyes.

    B. When a sick person is dying, he
stands above his pillow, with his sword
drawn in his hand, with a drop of gall
hanging on it. When the sick person
sees it, he trembles and gasps in fright,
and the angel then drops the drop into
his mouth, and from that drop the sick
person dies, from that drop the corpse
deteriorates, from that drop the face
becomes green.

7. A. [In the cases cited above], the woman
had just turned the corner [so it was by
accident that the sage saw her].

    8. A. "or at a woman's exquisite
clothing:"

    B. Said R. Judah said Samuel, "Even
if they are spread out on the wall."

    C. Said R. Pappa, "But that is only if
he knows who owns the clothing."

    D. *Said Raba, "You may derive that fact
from the wording, which is, 'a woman's
exquisite clothing,' and not 'exquisite
clothing' [in general]."*

    E. *That proves the point.*

    F. *Said R. Hisda, "That ruling applies
only if the clothing had been worn, but if*

the clothing is new, it does not matter.
For if you do not take that position, then
how can a woman's dresses be handed
over to a trimmer, who has to look at
them?"

G. *But in accord with your reasoning,*
how will you account for the position of
R. Judah that, in the case of animals of
the same species, one may bring
them together for mating by using a
tube [to insert the male's penis into
the female's vagina]? *He too has to*
look!

H. *The point of course is that at issue is*
simply doing the work with which he is
involved, and here too the answer is the
same.

9. A. The master has said, "and
from that drop the sick person dies:"

B. Shall we say that this statement
differs from the position of the father
of Samuel, for said the father of
Samuel, "The angel of death told me,
'If it were not for my respect for the
honor owing to people, I would cut the
throat of a man as broadly as the throat
of an animal' [so there really is an
incision, not merely a drop of bile]'"?

C. *Perhaps it is that very drop that cuts*
into the organs of the throat.

10. A. "from that drop the corpse
deteriorates:"

B. *This supports the view of R. Hanina bar Kahana, for said R. Hanania bar Kahana say the members of the household of Rab,* "He who wants a corpse not to deteriorate should turn it over on its face."

11. A. *Our rabbis have taught on Tannaite authority:*

B. "You shall keep yourself from every evil thing" (Dt. 23:10): one should not fantasize by day and so produce a nocturnal emission.

C. *In this connection* **said R. Phineas b. Yair, "Heedfulness leads to cleanliness, cleanliness leads to cleanness, cleanness leads to abstinence, abstinence leads to holiness, holiness leads to modesty, modesty leads to the fear of sin, the fear of sin leads to piety, piety leads to the Holy Spirit, the Holy Spirit leads to the resurrection of the dead, and the resurrection of the dead comes through Elijah, blessed be his memory [M. Sot. 9:15MM]** but piety is the greatest of these, as it is said, 'Then did you speak in a vision to your pious ones' (Ps. 89:20)."

D. *That differs from the opinion of R. Joshua b. Levi, for* said R. Joshua b. Levi, "Humility is the greatest of them all, for it is said, 'The spirit of the Lord God is upon me, because the Lord has anointed me to bring good tidings to the humble' (Is. 61:1). What Scripture says is not 'to the pious' but 'to the humble,' so humility is the greatest of these."

I.1 opens with a standard exegetical question on the scriptural basis for the Mishnah's law. As noted, the question that is answered is the scriptural basis for M. 1:8F–9: why not rent them houses and the like? No. 2 goes back over the ground of no. 1. Nos. 3 and 4 then form footnotes to nos. 1–2. No. 5, completed at no. 7, is a footnote to no. 4; nos. 6 and 8, to no. 5. Nos. 9 and 10 footnote no. 6. No. 11 then continues the exposition of Dt. 23:10, a footnote along with no. 6 to no. 5. The upshot is that the entire passage forms a cogent composite, answering a single question concerning the Mishnah paragraph, then glossing and amplifying the answer.

The principal chapter in Mishnah criticism—the Bavli's authors' favorite and recurrent interest—is devoted to the proposition that the Mishnah contains no contradictions among its laws, on the one side, and that the Mishnah never repeats the same point, on the other. The perfection of writing then replicates the flawless character of thought: consistency, on the one side, purposive discourse throughout, on the other; never contradiction, never repetition. These obvious components of an apologetic for the Mishnah based on the document's own traits of perfection generate a major part of the systematic program of the Talmud in its

address to the Mishnah. A striking expression of
the matter occurs at Mishnah-tractate Abodah Za-
rah 1:1 Bavli pericope II.1:

1:1

A. [2A] **Before the festivals of gentiles for
three days it is forbidden to do business with
them.**

B. **(1) to lend anything to them or to borrow
anything from them.**

C. **(2) to lend money to them or to borrow
money from them.**

D. **(3) to repay them or to be repaid by them.**

E. **R. Judah says, "They accept repayment
from them, because it is distressing to him."**

F. **They said to him, "Even though it is
distressing to him now, he will be happy
about it later."**

II.1 A. **Before the festivals of gentiles for
three days it is forbidden to do business with
them:**

B. *Do we impose so considerable a requirement?
Have we not learned in the Mishnah:* **At four
seasons in the year does he who sells a beast
to his fellow have to inform him [the
purchaser, so as to avoid violating the rule
against slaughtering the mother and the
offspring on the same day], "Its mother did I
sell for slaughter, its daughter did I sell for
slaughter," and these are they: (1) On the eve
of the last festival day of the Festival [of
Sukkot; (2) on the eve of the festival day of
Passover; (3) on the eve of Aseret [Shabuot],**

(4) and on the eve of the New Year. And in accord with the opinion of R. Yosé the Galilean, "Also on the eve of the Day of Atonement in Galilee." Said R. Judah, "Under what circumstances? When there is no space of time [between sales]. But if there is a space of time [between sales] he does not need to inform him. And R. Judah agrees in the case of one who sells the dam to the bridegroom and the daughter to the bride, that he needs to inform him, for it is certain that both will slaughter [them] on the same day [M. Hul. 5:3R–V]. [A single day's notice suffices, so why three days?]

C. *In that case, in which case the sale is for food, a single day's notice suffices. But here, since the sale is for making an offering, we require three days' notice.*

D. *But then are three days' notice sufficient in the case of the sale of an animal for an offering? And has it not been taught on Tannaite authority:* Questions are received concerning the laws of Passover prior to the Passover festival for a period of thirty days. Rabban Simeon b. Gamaliel says, "Two weeks."

E. [These questions are assumed to pertain to disqualifying blemishes affecting Passover offerings, and it follows,] since in our case blemishes that disqualify a beast are many, for we may disqualify a beast from serving as an offering even on account of a blemish on the eyelid, we require thirty days; but gentiles, who take account in that same connection only of the lack of a limb, will suffice with three days.

F. For, said R. Eleazar, "How on the basis of Scripture do we know that an animal that is lacking a limb may not be used by the children of Noah as a sacrifice? Since it is written, 'Of every living thing of all flesh two of every sort shall you bring into the ark' (Gen. 6:19). The Torah has said, therefore, 'Present as an offering beasts the principal limbs of which still are vital.'"

G. *But is that verse not required to eliminate from use for an offering a terefah-beast [one mortally wounded, which may not be eaten] indicating that they were not to be [brought into the ark]?*

H. *The exclusion of a terefah-beast is indicated by the statement,* "to keep seed alive" (Gen. 7:3).

I. *That judgment poses no problem to him who maintains that a terefah-beast cannot give birth.* **[6A]** *But in the opinion of him who maintains that a terefah-beast cannot give birth, what is there to say?*

J. Scripture has said, "[you shall bring] with you" (meaning, creatures that are like you [that is, whole in all limbs].

K. *But isn't it possible that Noah himself was in the classification of a terefah-creature [in that he may have carried some life-threatening ailment]?*

L. *Not at all, for in his regard it is written,* "perfect" (Gen. 6:9).

M. *But perhaps the reference to "perfect"*
(Gen. 6:9) *pertains to his deeds?*

N. In his regard "righteous" is *written
as well [and that covers the deeds].*

O. *But perhaps he was "perfect" in his*
ways, "righteous" in his deeds?

P. *Perish the thought that Noah might have
been a terefah-creature in his physical being,
for if you should imagine that Noah was a
terefah-creature then would the All-Merciful
have instructed him to present creatures like
himself and not to offer whole ones?*

Q. *Then if we derive that rule from the
language,* "with you" *meaning* "like you,"
what need is there for the reference to "to
keep seed alive" (Gen. 7:3)?

R. *Had the rule derived only from the
language,* "with you," *meaning* "like you,"
*I might have that that reference was made to
animals that serve just for company in general,
even a superannuated beast, and even a
castrated beast [would be fine for the ark].
When Scripture states,* "to keep seed alive"
(Gen. 7:3), [it eliminates that possible
conception].

The issue here is the harmonization of two Mishnah rules, which seem to exhibit conflicting premises. The solution is complete. As a matter of
fact, from F onward, we are given a sustained inquiry into the scriptural foundations for not our
Mishnah's rule but that of the intersecting one. But
the passage should be seen as unitary.

Just as the Mishnah in its anonymous and authoritative statements may not contain the imperfections of inconsistency, so the authorities of the Mishnah—Tannaite figures—also may not contradict themselves. An example of the Mishnah's interest in showing that Tannaite figures do not contradict themselves is at the following:

1:1

A. **[2A] Before the festivals of gentiles for three days it is forbidden to do business with them.**

B. **(1) to lend anything to them or to borrow anything from them.**

C. **(2) to lend money to them or to borrow money from them.**

D. **(3) to repay them or to be repaid by them.**

E. **R. Judah says, "They accept repayment from them, because it is distressing to him."**

F. **They said to him, "Even though it is distressing to him now, he will be happy about it later."**

VI.1 A. **R. Judah says, "They accept repayment from them, because it is distressing to him." They said to him, "Even though it is distressing to him now, he will be happy about it later:"**

B. *Now does R. Judah not accept the principle,* **"Even though it is distressing to him now, he will be happy about it later"?** *And has it not been taught on Tannaite authority:*

D. R. Judah says, "A woman should not put lime on her face on the intermediate days of a festival, since it makes her ugly." But R. Judah concedes that if the lime can be scraped off during the intermediate days of the festival, she may put it on during those same intermediate days, for **even though it is distressing to her now, she will be happy about it later."** [There is therefore a contradiction between the two rulings in Judah's name.]

E. Said R. Nahman bar Isaac, "Forget about the laws of the intermediate days of the festival, for all of them fall into the category, **'Even though it is distressing to him now, he will be happy about it later.'** "

F. *Rabina said, "As to a gentile, so far as getting repaid is concerned, it is always a source of anguish."*

Here again the point is that Judah is consistent in regard to the operative consideration. What he says in the Mishnah is wholly in accord with opinions assigned to him in other authoritative statements.

How about the other principal imperfection that can have been interpreted as a blemish on the document, I mean, repetition? A premise at the deepest layers of thought about the Mishnah (and Scripture) held that perfect writing never is redundant or repeats itself. Here is a case in which the Mishnah's repetition of the same principle through a number of cases leads to the suspicion that the document's framers needlessly repeat themselves. Accordingly, the theory of the perfection of the

Mishnah, advanced implicitly in the Talmud, requires us to show that every case is necessary, and the rule governing all cases cannot have been reasonably derived from any single one of them; each bears traits that distinguish it from all the others.

III.1 A. **to lend anything to them or to borrow anything from them:**

B. *There is no problem understanding why it is forbidden to lend them anything, because that gives them benefit. But as to borrowing from them, that serves to diminish [their capital]?*

C. *Said Abayye,"We forbid borrowing from them as a precautionary decree against the possibility of lending to them."*

D. *Raba said, "The entire consideration throughout is that he may go and give thanks for the transaction."*

IV.1 A. **to lend money to them or to borrow money from them:**

B. *There is no problem understanding why it is forbidden to lend them money, because that gives them benefit. But as to borrowing from them, that serves to diminish [their capital]?*

C. *Said Abayye, "We forbid borrowing from them as a precautionary decree against the possibility of lending to them."*

D. *Raba said, "The entire consideration throughout is that he may go and give thanks for the transaction."*

V.1 A. **to repay them or to be repaid by them:**

B. *There is no problem understanding why it is forbidden to repay money to them, because that gives them benefit. But as to borrowing from them, that serves to diminish [their capital]?*

C. *Said Abayye, "We forbid getting repaid by them as a precautionary decree against the possibility of repaying them."*

D. *Raba said, "The entire consideration throughout is that he may go and give thanks for the transaction."*

2. A. *And all the several instances are absolutely required.*

B. *For if the Tannaite authority had stated the rule only concerning doing business with them, that would be because the operative consideration is that they benefit from the transaction, so they will go and give thanks, but as to borrowing from them, which diminishes them, I might have said that that is acceptable.*

C. *And if the Tannaite authority had spoken only of borrowing from them, it is because that would involve something of importance to the other [knowing that the Jew needs to object], so he might go and give thanks for that, but as to borrowing money from him, which might cause only anxiety, since he might fear, "My money is not going to come back to me," [I might have supposed that that would be permitted.]*

D. *And if the Tannaite authority were to speak only of the case of lending money, that might be because the other might say, "I can forcibly collect," so he might have a fine reason to give thanks, but to recover money from them, which the lender might never otherwise get back, we might regard that as a source of trouble, in which case he would not give thanks for such a transaction. So all three cases are necessary.*

As we see, the Mishnah's several clauses are repetitiously explained, but then shown to complement one another and not to repeat the same point three times.

A subdivision of the interest in the matter of contradictions within positions held by a given authority finds definition into which authority will *not* concur with a given Mishnah rule. A very common point of inquiry will be how a named figure cannot accord with a rule, because an opinion he holds in some other matter altogether yields a contradictory premise. Then the effort will be made either to harmonize his view with the one at hand, or to admit that he may differ, because a figure who holds an opinion opposite to his at the other matter altogether will concur here; then we have a contradiction that is acceptable, that is, one between two named authorities. That is disagreement on principle, not a conflict of principles not assigned to a named authority and therefore taken to represent the consensus of sages as a whole, and that sort of conflict would profoundly blemish the document. Here is how we investigate the dissent a named figure would enter against our Mishnah rule—if he were to rule on the case before us.

1:1

A. [2A] **Before the festivals of gentiles for**

three days it is forbidden to do business with them.

B. (1) to lend anything to them or to borrow anything from them.

C. (2) to lend money to them or to borrow money from them.

D. (3) to repay them or to be repaid by them.

E. R. Judah says, "They accept repayment from them, because it is distressing to him."

F. They said to him, "Even though it is distressing to him now, he will be happy about it later."

Mishnah 1:1. VI.2.A *Our Mishnah passage does not accord with the position of R. Joshua b. Qorhah, for it has been taught on Tannaite authority:*

B. R. Joshua b. Qorha says, "In the case of any loan secured by a bond, one does not accept repayment from [a gentile] [M. 1:1D]. But in the case of any loan which is not secured by a bond, one does accept repayment from [a gentile], because one thereby saves the capital from their power" [T. 1:1H–K].

C. R. Joseph was in session behind R. Abba, with R. Abba in session facing R. Huna, who, in session, said, *"The law accords with R. Joshua b. Qorhah, and the law accords with R. Judah.*

D. *"The law accords with R. Joshua b. Qorhah in the case that we have just stated.*

E. *"and the law accords with R. Judah in the case in which we have learned in the Mishnah:* [If he gave wool to a dyer] to dye it red, and he dyed it black, [or] to dye it black, and he dyed it red—[7A] R. Meir says, '[The dyer] pays him back the value of his wool.' R. Judah says, 'If the increase in value is greater than the outlay for the process of dyeing, [the owner] pays him back the outlay for the process of dyeing. And if the outlay for the process of dyeing is greater than the increase in the value of the wool, [the dyer] pays him only the increase in value of the wool' [M. B. Q. 9:4G–K]."

F. *R. Joseph turned his face away: [in disgust, stating,] "Now a statement that the law accords with R. Joshua b. Qorhah was entirely in order. For you might have imagined that one might say,* where there is an individual opposed to the majority, the law accords with the position of the majority. *Here therefore we are informed that* the law follows the individual. *But why in the world should I have to be told that* the decided law accords with the position of R. Judah? *That is perfectly obvious. For where you have a dispute and then a statement of the law without attribution to a named authority, the decided law follows the unattributed formulation of the law. Now in point of fact, there is a dispute in Mishnah-tractate Baba Qama, while the law is presented without a named authority behind it in tractate Baba Mesia, for we have learned in the Mishnah:* **Whoever changes [the original terms of the agreement]—his hand is on the bottom. And whoever retracts—his hand is on the bottom [M. B. M. 6:2E–H].**"

G. And R. Huna?

H. *"The operative consideration here is that there is
no such fixed order to Mishnah-tractates. For one
might claim, quite to the contrary, that to begin
with the Tannaite framer of the document first of all
gave the law without an assigned authority, and
then he presented it as subject to dispute."*

I. *If so, in the case of any matter where* first of all
there is a dispute and afterward an
unattributed statement of the law, *one might
claim just as well, there is no such fixed order to
Mishnah-tractates.*

J. And R. Huna?

K. *When we invoke the principle that there is no
fixed order to the Mishnah, that concerns [the
contents of] a single tractate, but in respect to two
or more tractates, we do invoke that principle.*

L. And R. Joseph?

M. *The whole of the [three principal] tractates of
Damages [Baba Qamma, Baba Mesia, and Baba
Batra] are classified as a single tractate.*

N. *But if you prefer, I shall say, the reason is
that this rule is stated as a final decision, in this
language, after all:* **Whoever changes [the
original terms of the agreement]—his
hand is on the bottom. And whoever
retracts—his hand is on the bottom [M. B. M.
6:2E–H].**

The proposition is specific, but the premise, which
is demonstrated time and again, encompasses the
authorities of the document and shows that the
writing, and the writers, never err through inconsistency. Here is yet another example of how we

raise the question of whether the premise or implication of one Mishnah rule contradicts that of another, and we show that there is no contradiction
between them.

1:6

A. [15B] **In a place in which they are
accustomed to sell small cattle to gentiles,
they sell them.**
B. **In a place in which they are accustomed
not to sell [small cattle] to them, they do not
sell them.**
I.1 A. *Does this rule then bear the implication that
there is no real prohibition involved, but that it is
only a matter of custom, so that where it is
customary to prohibit selling them, it is prohibited,
and where it is customary to permit selling to them,
it is permitted? And an objection is to be raised:*
**They do not leave cattle in gentiles' inns,
because they are suspect in regard to bestiality
[M. 2:1A–B].**
B. Said Rab, "In a place in which it is
permitted to sell beasts to them, it is permitted
to leave them alone together with beasts, and
in a place in which it is forbidden to leave
them alone with beasts, it also is customarily
forbidden also to sell beasts to them [and both
passages depend on local custom]."
C. **[15A]** And R. Eleazar says, "Even in a place
in which it is forbidden to leave a gentile alone
with a beast, it is permitted to sell the beast to
him. *What is the operative consideration? The*

155

gentile is concerned that his beast not be
hamstrung."
D. *And also Rab retracted his ruling, for R.*
Tahalipa said R. Shila bar Abimi said in the name of
Rab, "The gentile is concerned that his beast
not be hamstrung."

The solution the the proposed contradiction is
fully exposed here. In line with the argument
spelled out earlier, I give the following instance of
the harmonization of conflict so that secondary materials, such as footnotes or appendices, are set off
from what is primary to the Talmud's discussion—
but nonetheless required by it.

1:7

A. **They do not sell them (1) bears or (2)**
lions, or (3) anything which is a public
danger.
I.1 A. Said R. Hanina b. R. Hisda, and some
say, said R. Hanan b. Raba in the name of
Rab, "To large cattle the same rule applies as
to small cattle when it comes to the criterion of
struggling, [specifically, that, after slaughter,
the animal must show signs of struggling to be
fit for food; otherwise we assume it died prior
to slaughter and is carrion; the struggle in the
case of small cattle must be stretching out and
bending back of a leg, in the case of large
cattle, one or the other]. But that is not the
case when it comes to selling the beast [which
is governed by local custom]. But, for my part,
I say that the same is so even in regard to

selling: in a place in which it is customary to sell such beasts, they sell them, and if it is customary not to sell such beasts, they do not sell them."

B. *We have learned in the Mishnah:* **They do not sell them (1) bears or (2) lions, or (3) anything which is a public danger.** *Therefore the operative consideration is danger to the public. So if there is no danger to the public, then there is no objection to selling such beasts to them [contrary to Rab's opinion].*

C. Said Rabbah bar Ulla, "Our Mishnah deals with a mutilated lion, and that is in accord with the opinion of R. Judah **[R. Judah permits doing so in the case of a lame one, which is not subject to healing (M. 1:6D)].**

D. Said R. Ashi, "Any lion, so far as actually working with it, is deemed 'mutilated.' "

E. *An objection was raised from the following:* **And just as they do not sell them a large domesticated beast, so they do not sell them a large wild beast [M. 1:6B]. And also in a situation in which they do not sell them a small domesticated beast, they do not sell them a small wild beast. [T. A. Z. 2:2].** *Does this not refute the opinion of R. Hanan b. Raba [who permits doing so if it is customary]?*

F. *It does indeed refute that opinion.*

2. A. *Rabina contrasted a Mishnah teaching with a Tannaite teaching external to the Mishnah and he resolved the contradiction: "We have learned in the Mishnah:* **They do not sell them (1) bears or (2) lions, or (3) anything which is a public**

danger. *The operative consideration then is that these constitute a public danger. Lo, if there is no danger to the public, they may sell such beasts to gentiles. And by contrast:* **And just as they do not sell them a large domesticated beast, so they do not sell them a large wild beast [M. 1:6B].** **And also in a situation in which they do not sell them a small domesticated beast, they do not sell them a small wild beast [T. A. Z. 2:2].** *Now he further harmonized these two teachings: the Mishnah refers to a mutilated lion, and accords with the view of R. Judah."*

B. Said R. Ashi, "Any lion, so far as actually working with it, is deemed 'mutilated.'

C. *R. Nahman objected, "Who is going to tell us that a lion is classified as a large beast? Perhaps it is classified as a small one?"*

D. *R. Ashi subjected our Mishnah paragraph to a close reading and replied to the objection with a refutation: "We have learned in the Mishnah,* **They do not sell them (1) bears or (2) lions, or (3) anything which is a public danger.** *The operative consideration then is that these constitute a public danger. Lo, if there is no danger to the public, they may sell such beasts to gentiles. And the operative consideration involving a lion is,* Any lion, so far as actually working with it, is deemed 'mutilated.' But anything else that is fit for labor would not be subject to that prohibition. *Does this not refute the opinion of R. Hanan b. Raba?"*

E. *It does indeed refute that opinion.*

3. A. And as to a large wild beast, to what sort of labor is it suited?

B. Said Abayye, "Said Mar Judah to me, 'At the household of Mar Yohani, they work mills with wild asses.' "

4. A. Said R. Zira, "When we were at the household of R. Judah, he said to us, 'Learn from me the following statement, for I have heard it from a preeminent authority, though I do not know whether it was from Rab or from Samuel:

B. " 'As to large wild beasts, the same rule applies as to small cattle when it comes to the criterion of struggle, [specifically, that, after slaughter, the animal must show signs of struggling to be fit for food; otherwise we assume it died prior to slaughter and is carrion; the struggle in the case of small cattle must be stretching out and bending back of a leg, in the case of large cattle, one or the other].'

C. "Now when I came to Qurdeqonia, I found R. Hiyya bar Ashi, who was in session and making the following statement in the name of Samuel: 'As to large wild beasts, the same rule applies as to small cattle when it comes to the criterion of struggling.' And I said to myself, 'That means that it has been stated in the name of Samuel.'

D. "But when I came to Sura, I found Rabbah bar Jeremiah in session and stating the same thing in the name of Rab: 'As to

large wild beasts, the same rule applies as to
small cattle when it comes to the criterion of
struggling.' And I said to myself, 'That
means that it has been stated in the name of
Rab and it has also been stated in the name
of Samuel.'

E. "Moreover, when I went up there [to the
Land of Israel], I found R. Assi in session
and stating, 'Said R. Hama bar Guria in the
name of Rab: "As to large wild beasts, the
same rule applies as to small cattle when it
comes to the criterion of struggling." ' I said
to him, 'Do you not take the view, then,
that the one who reported this teaching in
the name of Rab is Rabbah b. Jeremiah?'

F. "And he said to me, 'Black pot! Through
me and through you will this report be
completed' [Mishcon: Hama heard it from
Rab, and Rabbah heard it reported from
Hama]."

G. *So it has been stated also:* Said R. Zira said
R. Assi said Rabbah bar Jeremiah said Rab
Hama bar Guria said Rab, "As to large wild
beasts, the same rule applies as to small
cattle when it comes to the criterion of
struggling."

No. 4 simply goes over an established discussion,
making no new point but providing a richer account of the same issue. The whole, a single composite, serves the purpose of showing that there is
no disharmony between the Mishnah's rule and
that which is found in another Tannaite source.

1:7

A. They do not sell them (1) bears or (2) lions, or (3) anything which is a public danger.

B. They do not build with them (1) a basilica, (2) scaffold, (3) stadium, or (4) judges' tribunal.

II.1 A. They do not build with them (1) a basilica, (2) scaffold, (3) stadium, or (4) judges' tribunal:

B. Said Rabbah b. Bar Hanna said R. Yohanan, "There are three classifications of basilicas: those belonging to gentile kings, those belonging to bathhouses, and those belonging to store houses."

C. Said Raba, "Two of those are permitted, the third forbidden [for Israelite workers to build], and your mnemonic is 'to bind their kings with chains' (Ps. 149:8).

D. And there are those who say, said Raba, "All of them are permitted [for Israelite workers to build]."

E. *But have we not learned in the Mishnah:* **They do not build with them (1) a basilica, (2) scaffold, (3) stadium, or (4) judges' tribunal?**

F. *Say that that rule applies in particular to* a basilica to which is attached an executioner's scaffold, a stadium, or a judge's tribunal.

II.1 accomplishes the same purpose, of harmonizing opinions. Because of II.1, II.2 is tacked on. We have already considered the entire composite.

Consistency is shown to characterize not only
the authorities of the Mishnah in their reading of
the Mishnah, but also the masters of the Tosefta.
At issue then is not a particular piece of writing,
though that formed the precipitating question, but
the authorities themselves, whether their sayings
occur in the Mishnah or in some other document
identified by us or in a documentary context un-
known to us but simply classified as Tannaite. In
the following, we find Tannaite materials not in the
Mishnah subjected to the familiar process of harmonization. Once more I indent what I deem to be
footnotes, appendices, and other subordinated
materials, which find a place within the larger composite.

> **Mishnah Abodah Zarah 1:7** III.1 A. *Our rabbis*
> *have taught on Tannaite authority:*
> B. **He who goes to a stadium or to a camp to**
> **see the performances of sorcerers and**
> **enchanters or of various kinds of clowns,**
> **mimics, buffoons, and the like—lo, this is a**
> *seat of the scoffers,* **as it is said, "Happy is the**
> **man who has not walked in the counsel of the**
> **wicked . . . nor sat in the seat of the scoffers.**
> **But his delight is in the Torah of the Lord"**
> **(Ps. 1:12). Lo, you thereby learn that these**
> **things cause a man to neglect the study of the**
> **Torah [T. A. Z. 2:6A–D].**
> C. *An objection was raised on the basis of the*
> *following:* **[Following Tosefta's wording:] He**
> **who goes up into gentiles' amphitheaters, if**
> **he was going about on account of the service**

of the state's requirements, lo, this is permitted. If one takes account [of what is happening therein], lo, this is forbidden. [He who sits in an amphitheater [e.g., where gladiators are fighting], lo, this one is guilty of bloodshed. R. Nathan permits on two counts: because [the Israelite] cries out in order to save the life [of the loser], and because he may give evidence in behalf of a woman [whose husband is killed in the struggle], that she may remarry.] They may go to stadiums because [an Israelite] will cry out in order to save the life of the loser, [and to the performance in a camp on account of the task of preserving order in the province. But if one takes account of what is happening [in the entertainment], lo, this forbidden] [T. A. Z. 2:7A–I].

D. *So there is a contradiction as to laws on stadiums and a contradiction as to laws on military camps.*

E. *There is in point of fact no contradiction as to the rules governing military camps, for the one speaks of a case in which he conspires with them, the other, where he does not. But there is a contradiction as to the laws on going to stadiums.*

F. *In point of fact it represents a conflict of opinion between two Tannaite authorities, for it has been taught on Tannaite authority:*

G. One may not go to a stadium because it is a 'seat of scorners.'

H. R. Nathan permits doing so on two counts: because [the Israelite] cries out in order to

save the life [of the loser], and because he
may give evidence in behalf of a woman
[whose husband is killed in the struggle], that
she may remarry.

2. A. *Our rabbis have taught on Tannaite
authority:*

B. "People may not go to theaters or circuses
for there they 'make dung' for idolatry," the
words of R. Meir.

C. And sages say, "In a place in which they
'make dung' for idolatry, it is forbidden by
reason of suspicion that idolatry is taking
place, but in a place in which they do not
'make dung' for idolatry, it is permitted."

D. *What is at issue between these two opinions?*

E. Said R. Hanina, "At issue between them is
whether or not to go to do business [and if
there is no idolatry sages would not forbid
going to the stadium]."

What has been said suffices to demonstrate the
first proposition of perfection: the document is perfect in that it rests upon Scripture and exhibits no
flaws of inconsistency. But the implicit proposition
is that the authorities cited in the Mishnah and in
compilations of equivalent authority likewise stand
upon the authority of Sinai and in no way contradict themselves; and the anonymous law, which is
to be obeyed, is wholly harmonious.

The inquiry into the perfect consistency of the
Mishnah and also of its authorities yielded a fur-
ther search, one into the premise of a given rule.
For knowing the reason for a rule of the Mishnah

would allow us to move from one topic to another, in which the same underlying reason yielded a rule upon an entirely unrelated topic. Then if we can show that the premise of one ruling contradicts the premise of another, unrelated ruling, we can challenge the prevailing claim of perfection. As an apologetic document, the Bavli employs a hermeneutic in which a principal precipitant of Mishnah exegesis in the Bavli is the question of the harmony of the deep premises of rulings that on the surface do not intersect. And this may or may not yield a further inquiry, e.g., into the relationshp between two distinct rules, each of which may turn out to appeal to a shared premise or a contradictory one (as already noted].

Here is a fine example of a sustained inquiry into the operative considerations behind a rule of a Mishnah paragraph. What we see is how that inquiry draws our attention to laws on other subjects entirely, which rest on, or imply, principles shared with the passage under discussion.

1:6

A. **In a place in which they are accustomed to sell small cattle to gentiles, they sell them.**

B. **In a place in which they are accustomed not to sell [small cattle] to them, they do not sell them.**

C. **And in no place do they sell them large cattle, calves, or foals, whether whole or lame.**

D. **R. Judah permits in the case of lame ones.**

E. **And Ben Beterah permits in the case of a horse.**

II.1 A. **And in no place do they sell them large cattle, calves, or foals, whether whole or lame:**

B. *What is the operative consideration here?*

C. *Granted that we do not take precautions against the possibility of bestiality, we do take account of the consideration of the gentile's making the animal work on the Sabbath.*

D. *So let him work the beast! Since he bought it, he has acquired title to it.*

E. *We decree against selling it to gentiles on account of the consideration of his possibly lending it out or renting it out.*

F. *But if he lends it out or rents it out, still, during that span of time, he owns the beast!*

G. *Rather, said Rami b. R. Yeba, "It is a decree on account of the possibility of someone's [experimenting in the process of] assessing how much the beast can hold. For on occasions he might sell him the beast close to sunset on the Sabbath evening, and the gentile may say to him, 'Come and let us see how much it can bear,' and when the beast hears the owner's voice, it will walk because of him, and the Israelite wants it to walk, so on the Sabbath he turns out to act as the driver of his loaded-up beast,* and he who [not intending to violate the Sabbath] on the Sabbath drives his loaded up beast is [nonetheless] liable to bring a sin offering."

H. *Objected R. Shisha b. Idi, "But, furthermore, does one who hires out the beast acquire title to it?*

And have we not learned in the Mishnah: **Even in
the situation concerning which they have
ruled [that they may] rent, it is not for use as
a residence that they ruled that it is permitted,
because he brings an idol into it.** *Now should it
enter your mind that one who rents thereby acquires
title, in this case, if he brings in an idol, he brings
it into his own house anyhow!"*

I. *The case of an idol is exceptional, because it is
subject to a very strict rule, as it is written, "And
you shall not bring abomination into your
house" (Dt. 7:26).*

J. *Objected R. Isaac b. R. Mesharshayya, "But,
furthermore, does one who hires out a beast acquire
title to it? And lo, we have learned in the Mishnah:*
**An Israelite who hired a cow from a priest
may feed it vetches in the status of heave
offering. But a priest who hired a cow from
an Israelite, even though he is responsible for
feeding it, may not feed it vetches in the
status of heave offering [M. Ter. 11:9 C–F].** *[So
title has not been transferred either way.] Now
should it enter your mind that one who rents
thereby acquires title, in this case, why should he
not feed it produce in the status of heave offering? It
is, after all, his cow! Rather, that proves, renting
out a beast does not for that interval transfer title to
the beast."*

K. *Now that you have reached the position that
renting out the beast does not transfer title, the
decree prohibiting sale of large cattle to gentiles is
on the counts of both renting out the beast and also
because of lending the beast and also because of*

*trying the beast out to see how much a load it can
sustain.*

2. A. *R. Ada permitting selling an ass to a
heathen through an agent. As for the
consideration of trying out the beast to see how
much a load it can sustain, the beast will not
know the voice of the agent that it should walk
because of hearing it [so that consideration is
null]; as to the considerations of lending or hiring
it, since the beast is not the agent's, he will not
lend the beast nor give it over, lest some fault
turn up in it [and it is the agent's task to sell the
beast].*

3. A. *R. Huna sold a cow to a gentile. Said to
him R. Hisda, "How come the master has done
this?"*

B. *He said to him, "I take for granted that he
bought the beast to slaughter it for meat."*

C. **[15B]** *"And on what basis do you reach such
a conclusion in a case of this sort?"*

D. *"It is because we have learned in the
Mishnah:* **The House of Shammai say,
'During the Sabbatical year a person may
not sell to another a heifer used for
plowing.' But the House of Hillel permit
one to sell such a heifer because he [the
buyer] may slaughter it [M. Sheb. 5:8A–B].***"*

E. *Said Raba, "Are the two matters really
comparable at all? In that case* a person is
not subject to the religious duty of
securing Sabbath rest for his cattle in the
Sabbatical Year [so there is no issue of not
hiring, lending, or trying out the beast in

that connection when a gentile is concerned], *while in this case,* a person is subject to the religious duty of securing the Sabbath rest for his beast."

F. *Said to him Abayye, "But is it the fact that in any case in which one is so commanded, is such a sale prohibited? And lo, there is the case of the field, in which instance* a person is subject to the religious duty of securing the Sabbath rest for his field, *and yet we have learned:* **The House of Shammai say, 'A person may not sell a plowed field in the Sabbatical year.' And the House of Hillel permit, because it is possible that he will still let it lie fallow'** [T. Shebiit 3:2]."

G. *Objected R. Ashi, "And is it the fact that in any case in which a person is not subject to a religious obligation, a deed is permitted in any event [so that one may sell the object to someone who is going to use the object contrary to that religious duty]? And lo, there is the case of utensils, concerning which a person is not subject to a religious duty to secure for them Sabbath rest in the Sabbatical Year, and yet we have learned in the Mishnah:* **These are tools which the artisan is not permitted to sell during the Sabbatical year: (1) a plow and all its accessories, (2) a yoke, (3) a pitchfork, (4) and a mattock. But he [the artisan] may sell: (1) a hand sickle, (2) a reaping sickle, (3) and a wagon and all its accessories. This is the**

> general rule: [as regards] any [tool] the
> use of which [during the Sabbatical year]
> is limited to a transgression—it is
> forbidden [to sell such a tool during the
> Sabbatical year]. [But as for any tool
> which may be used both for work which
> is] forbidden and [for work which is]
> permitted [according to the laws of the
> Sabbatical year—it is permissible to sell
> such a tool during the Sabbatical year]
> [M. Sheb. 5:6A–G]."
>
> H. *Rather, said R. Ashi, "In any case in
> which there is the possibility of assuming [that
> the beast will be properly used], we invoke that
> assumption, even though one is subject to a
> religious responsibility, but in any case in
> which there is no possibility of assuming that
> the beast will not be properly used, we do not
> invoke that assumption, even though there is
> no religious responsibility to which one is
> subject."*

II.1 asks about the operative consideration for the Mishnah's rule. We rapidly move into the issue of ownership and transfer of title. Nos. 2 and 3 go on to cite precedents. No. 3 then leads us to a rule on another matter altogether, which links to the present case through a supposedly shared principle. These examples suffice to show how the infrastructure time and again bears the burden of a single message: the Mishnah is perfect.

Now to generalize: the Mishnah addresses the life of Israel, the holy people, and the Bavli, the Mishnah. The Mishnah forms the center of the Bavli's authors' attention, the precipitating focus of nearly the whole of the Bavli's inquiry. In describing, then interpreting, the testimony of the Talmud of Babylonia about the formation of Judaism, therefore, we must locate the points of insistence, the recurrent questions, the patterns of thought, which, all together, tell us *what*, about the Mishnah in particular. For the Mishnah's character confronted the Bavli's sages as the issue of urgency. Beyond the specificities of exegesis of the Mishnah lay the generality of their apologia for that writing. Their principal message concerning the Mishnah portrayed the Mishnah as a perfect piece of writing. By perfection these heirs of philosophy meant a document containing no imperfections of internal contradiction and disharmony, repetition and redundancy, flaws of poor or ambiguous formulation, but above all, damaging self-contradictions. They accepted that authorities might differ. But a given master had to be entirely consistent in everything he said. Assigned sayings might conflict with others of their class; but what was anonymous, therefore authoritative, everywhere had to cohere.

So the document, and the authorities for whom it stood, required the demonstration that the writing was perfect in its harmony and—it goes without saying—also entirely symmetrical with the written Torah, Scripture. These were points that, in vast detail, our sages of blessed memory made

171

whenever they proposed to compose a discourse.[9] So while the Mishnah's ubiquitously demonstrated proposition present in most detailed expositions set forth in all things the hierarchical classification of all being, the Bavli's counterpart concerned the perfection of the document itself. But, of course, showing the harmony of a piece of writing imposed disciplines of thought—rational analysis, regulated representation of evidence, reasoned argument—which governed thought throughout.

---

9. I do not maintain that these were the only points which sages wished repeatedly to register. I do not know all of those things that they wished to say through many things. But the one thing set forth here certainly enjoyed the highest priority.

Part Four

Talmudic Thinking and the Social World of Judaism

Chapter 5

Writing and the Social Order

The Talmud speaks in a single voice. Everywhere, uniformly, consistently, and predictably, resonates the voice of a book. The message is one deriving from a community, the collectivity of sages for whom and to whom the book speaks. The document seems, in the main, to intend to provide notes, an abbreviated script which anyone may use to reconstruct and reenact formal discussions of problems: about this, one says that. Curt and often arcane, these notes can be translated only with immense bodies of inserted explanation. All of this script of information is public and undifferentiated, not individual and idiosyncratic. We must assume people took for granted that, out of the signs of speech, it would be possible for anyone to reconstruct speech, doing so in accurate and fully conventional ways. So the literary traits of the document presuppose a uniform code of communication: a single voice.

The Talmud of Babylonia line by line reveals a consistently coherent and harmonious document, one that has time and again moved from beginning to what was, in fact, a well-planned and predetermined end. The voice, the Bavli's one voice, rightly personified in the classical academies of Talmud study as simply "the Talmud," speaks to us throughout—the Talmud and not the diverse voices of real people engaged in a concrete and

therefore chaotic argument. As in Plato's dialogues, question and answer—the dialectical argument—constitute conventions through which
logic is exposed and tested, not the reports of
things people said spontaneously or even after the
fact. The controlling voice is monotonous, lacking
all points of differentiation of viewpoint, tone,
mode of inquiry, and thought.

So the Talmud is not a mere compilation of this
and that, the result of centuries of the accumulation, in a haphazard way, of the detritus of various
schools or opinions. The four pages of Bavli Baba
Mesia that we followed, beginning to end, have
shown us a sample of the Talmud that is exceedingly carefully and well crafted, a sustained and cogent inquiry. Scarcely a single line is out of place;
not a sentence in the entire passage sustains the
view of a document that is an agglutinative compilation. We can state very simply how the Talmud
analyzes our Mishnah passage. We begin with the
clarification of the Mishnah paragraph, turn then
to the examination of the principles of law implicit
in the Mishna paragraph, and then broaden the
discussion to introduce what I called analogies
from case to law and law to case. These are the
three stages of discussion. Within the protracted
discussion, we note numerous cross-references,
points made much earlier being reconsidered in a
fresh context. The various propositions were sys-
tematically tested and examined. If the passage
was orally formulated and orally transmitted, we
can discern, moreover, no indications of a mnemonic; the whole seems to presuppose the possi-

bility of cross-references, of referring later on to an earlier passage, and other indications of the premise of a written document or at least notes. It would be very easy to outline the discussion, beginning to end, and to produce a reasoned account of the position and order of every completed composition and the ordering of the several compositions into a composite. And that composite really does provide a beginning and an end.

The facts before us do not indicate a haphazard, episodic, sedimentary process of agglutination and conglomeration. They point, quite to the contrary, to a well-considered and orderly composition, planned from beginning to end and following an outline that is definitive throughout. That outline has told the framers of the passage what comes first—the simplest matters of language, then the more complex matters of analysis of content, then secondary development of analogous principles and cases. We do move from simple criticism of language to weighty analysis of parallels. True, we invoke facts treated elsewhere; but these are carefully footnoted, and while in form the footnotes disrupt the flow of argument, in substance a discerning student of the document readily follows the whole.

The Talmud's one voice is heard with great clarity, because the Talmud throughout, at every line, comprises a composition, not merely a compilation. We know that that is so, because of two facts. First, the Talmud's authors or authorship follow a few rules, which we can easily discern, in order to say everything they wish. So the document is uniform and rhetorically cogent. The highly orderly and systematic character of the Talmud emerges, first of all, in the regularities of language, as we saw in part 1. All data unite to form a cogent composite, on a single subject, making a single large point, as shown in part 2. And, as part 3 has shown, the Talmud speaks through one voice, that voice of logic which with vast assurance reaches into our own minds and, by asking the logical and urgent next question, tells us what we should be thinking. And that turns out to be a single point, made in many ways over and over again. So the Talmud's rhetoric seduces us into joining its analytical inquiry, always raising precisely the question that should trouble us.

The Talmud speaks about the Mishnah in essentially a single voice, about fundamentally few things. Its languages, its logic of the coherence of composites, its recurrent, single law shown beyond explication of many laws all work together. Its mode of speech as much as of thought is uniform throughout. Diverse topics produce slight differentiation in modes of analysis. The same sorts of questions phrased in the same rhetoric—a moving, or dialectical, argument, composed of questions and answers—turn out to pertain equally well to every subject and problem. The Talmud's discourse forms a closed system in which people say the same thing about everything. The fact that the Talmud speaks in a single voice supplies striking evidence (1) that the Talmud does speak in particular for the age in which its units of discourse took shape, and (2) that that work was done toward the end of that long period of Mishnah reception that began at the end of the second century and came to an end at the conclusion of the sixth century. When the Talmud speaks about a passage of the Mishnah, it generally takes up a single, not very complex or diverse, program of inquiry. The Talmud also utilizes a single, rather limited repertoire of exegetical initiatives and rhetorical choices for whatever discourse about the Mishnah the framers of the Talmud propose to undertake. Accordingly, as is clear, the Talmud presents us with both a uniformity of discourse anad a monotony of tone. The Talmud speaks in a single voice. That voice by definition is collective, not greatly differentiated by traits of individuals.

When did the textual community for which the Talmud speaks do the work? The Talmudic unit of discourse approaches the explanation of a passage of the Mishnah without systematic attention to the layers in which ideas were set forth, the schools among which discussion must have been divided, the sequence in which statements about a Mishnah law were made. That fact points to formation at the end, not agglutination in successive layers of intellectual sediment. In a given unit of discourse, the focus, the organizing principle, the generative interest—these are defined solely by the issue at hand. The argument moves from point to point, directed by the inner logic of argument itself. A single plane of discourse is established. All things are leveled out, so that the line of logic runs straight and true. Accordingly, a single conception of the framing and formation of the unit of discourse stands prior to the spelling out of issues. More fundamental still, what people in general wanted was not to create topical anthologies—to put together instances of what this one said about that issue—but to exhibit the logic of that issue, viewed under the aspect of eternity. Under sustained inquiry we always find a theoretical issue, freed of all temporal considerations and the contingencies of politics and circumstances.

Once these elemental literary facts make their full impression, everything else falls into place as well. Arguments did not unfold over a long period of time, as one generation made its points, to be followed by the additions and revisions of another generation, in a process of gradual increment and agglutination running on for two hundred years. That theory of the formation of literature cannot account for the unity, stunning force, and dynamism of the Talmud's dialectical arguments. To the contrary, someone (or some small group) at the end determined to reconstruct, so as to expose, the naked logic of a problem. For this purpose, often, it was found useful to cite sayings or positions in hand from earlier times. But these inherited materials underwent a process of reshaping, and, more aptly, refocusing. Whatever the original words—and we need not doubt that at times we have them—the point of everything in hand was defined and determined by the people who made it all up at the end. The whole shows a plan and program. Theirs are the minds behind the whole. In the nature of things, they did their work at the end, not at the outset.

So the Talmud's one voice speaks in behalf of the textual community that wrote the Talmud: those who formed the composites that we have analyzed in these pages. It follows that the whole is the work of the one who decided to make up the discussion on the atemporal logic of the point at issue. Otherwise, the discussion would be not continuous but disjointed, full of seams and margins, marks of the existence of prior conglomerations of materials that have now been sewn together. What we have are not patchwork quilts, but woven fabric. Along these same lines, we may find discussions in which opinions of Palestinians, such as Yohanan and Simon b. Laqish, will be joined together side by side with opinions by Babylonians, such as Rab and Samuel. The whole, once again, will unfold in a smooth way, so that the issues at hand define the sole focus of discourse. The logic of those issues will be fully exposed. Considerations of the origin of a saying in one country or the other will play no role whatsoever in the rhetoric or literary forms of argument. There will be no possibility of differentiation among opinions on the basis of where, when, by whom, or how they are formulated, only the basis of what, in fact, is said.

Accordingly, the role of individuals is unimportant. Shared reason, not individual genius, governs throughout. The paramount voice is that of "the Talmud." The rhetoric of the Talmud may be described very simply: a preference for questions and answers, a willingness then to test the answers and to expand through secondary and tertiary amplification, achieved through further questions and answers. The whole gives the appearance of the script for a conversation to be reconstructed, or an argument of logical possibilities to be reenacted, in one's own mind. In this setting we of course shall be struck by the uniformity of the rhetoric, even though we need not make much of the close patterning of language. The voice of "the Talmud," moreover, authoritatively defines the mode of analysis. The inquiry is consistent and predictable; one argument differs from another not in supposition but only in detail. When individuals' positions occur, it is because what they have to say serves the purposes of "the Talmud" and its uniform inquiry. The inquiry is into the logic and the rational potentialities of a passage. To these dimensions of thought, the details of place, time, and even of an individual's philosophy, are secondary. All details are turned toward a common core of discourse. This, I maintain, is possible only because the document as a whole takes shape in accord with an overriding program of inquiry and comes to expression in conformity with a single plan of rhetorical expression. To state the proposition simply: it did not just grow, but rather, someone made it up.

The Talmudic argument is not indifferent to the chronology of authorities. But the sequence in which things may be supposed to have been said— an early third-century figure's saying before a later fourth-century figure's saying—in no way explains the construction of protracted dialectical arguments. The argument as a whole, its direction and purpose, always govern the selection, formation, and ordering of the parts of the argument and their relationships to one another. The dialectic is determinative. Chronology, if never violated, is always subordinated. Once that fact is clear, it will become further apparent that "arguments"—analytical units of discourse—took shape at the end, with the whole in mind, as part of a plan and a program. That is to say, the components of the argument, even when associated with the names of specific authorities who lived at different times, were not added piece by piece, in order of historical appearance. They were put together whole and complete, all at one time, when the dialectical discourse was made up. By examining a few units of discourse, we shall clearly see the unimportance of the sequence in which people lived, hence of the order in which sayings (presumably) became available.

The upshot is that chronological sequence, while not likely to be ignored, never determines the layout of a unit of discourse. We can never definitively settle the issue of whether a unit of discourse came into being through a long process of accumulation and agglutination, or was shaped at one point—then, at the end of the time in which named authorities flourished—with everything in hand and a particular purpose in mind. But the more likely of the two possibilities is clearly the latter. It seems to me likely that the purposes of dialectical argument determined not only which available sayings were selected for inclusion, but also the order and purpose in accordance with which sayings were laid out.

That is why, in my view, it follows that the whole—the unit of discourse as we know it, which I call the composite—was put together at the end. At that point everything was in hand, and so available for arrangement in accordance with a principle other than chronology, and in a rhetoric common to all sayings. That other principle will then have determined the arrangement, drawing in its wake resort to a single monotonous voice: "the Talmud." The principle is logical exposition, that is to say, the analysis and dissection of a problem into its conceptual components. The dialectic of argument is framed not by considerations of the chronological sequence in which sayings were said but by attention to the requirements of reasonable exposition of the problem. That is what governs.

In this regard, then, the Talmud is like the Mishnah in its fundamental literary traits, therefore also in its history. The Mishnah was formulated in its rigid, patterned language and carefully organized and enumerated groups of formal-substantive cognitive units, in the very processes in which it also was redacted. Otherwise, the correspondences between redactional program and formal and patterned mode of articulation of ideas cannot be explained, short of invoking the notion of a literary miracle. The Talmud too underwent a process of redaction, in which fixed and final units of discourse were organized and put together. The work, probably antecedent, of framing and formulating these units of discourse appears to have gone on at a single period, among a relatively small number of sages working within a uniform set of literary conventions, at roughly the same time, and in approximately the same way. The end product, the Talmud, like the Mishnah, is uniform and stylistically coherent, generally consistent in modes of thought and speech, wherever we turn. That accounts for the single voice that leads us through the dialectical and argumentative analysis of the Talmud. That voice is ubiquitous and insistent.

What I have tried to do in these pages is use my imagination to grasp in the broadest possible dimensions and explain in the most acute detail what problems the writers of the Talmud had to solve. The answers explain why these solutions achieved the success — intellectual and aesthetic, political and cultural alike — that they have for so many centuries. No writer ambitious to change the world through his words, as I am, can have missed the mystery of their success: through rationality, compellingly set forth, to form the world. And no concerned citizen reflecting upon the requirements of sustaining an orderly society of people left by limited government free to make up their own minds and exercise free and uncoerced choices, dictated only by reason, can have failed to admire this particular writing.

Unlike the writers to whom we referred at the outset, James Madison and Alexander Hamilton and the others who bear responsibility for the composition of the United States Constitution, the Talmud's authors and their heirs had no government to compel people to do what they said. And unlike Hamilton and Madison, its writers enjoyed no public position to lend weight and credence to their explanation. And, unlike the judges and senators and representatives, secretaries of state and war and treasury, its sponsors had only the standing which their own powers of persuasion could gain for them. Reason is the power of the weak; argument, the ultimate weapon of the powerless. Effective writing provides the ammunition of those who, like Israel, the people, before the state of Israel, could take aim only with self-evidently right arguments set forth in well-crafted sentences (of whatever, in context, these might consist). The Bavli teaches us never to underestimate the power of a well-drafted sentence.

The social order portrayed by the authors of the Bavli realized, in the well-written portrayal of what occupied mind and imagination, the world in which they, and (in their view) all Israel, wanted to make their lives. It was a domain in which reason mattered, argument bore weight, and rationality characterized everyday transactions and relationships. The Bavli's authors show, therefore, how intellectuals write out their fantasies in the form of effective prose for the function of dictating the composition of a composite society: utopian Israel, wherever and whenever they took their place. And the long and remarkably successful record of the Bavli in shaping the affairs of Israel portrays a society that realizes intellectuals' fantasies. Given the catastrophes that have overtaken humanity when other intellectuals' fantasies have taken over and formed reality—Plato's in fascism, for example, and Marx's in communism—our sages of blessed memory need not apologize for what they did to—

and also for—Israel the holy people. From the seventh to the twentieth century, their thought as they wrote it up governed the kingdom of philosophers, instructed through the power of persuasion the nation of priests, and compelled through sound argument, persuasively set forth, the holy people about the reasoned way of building the house of Israel. Wherever located, that house would be everywhere the same: utopian Parthenon of the spirit, perfect in the details of all proportions and intricate relationships, hierarchical classification of all being from its locus in any given here and now to that one, the eternal, in the heights. Such is the power of Talmudic thinking in its aspects of language, logic, and law.

General Index

Index of Biblical and
Talmudic References

DATE DUE

HIGHSMITH 45-220